The Householder's
Guide to Plumbing

JAMES M. HAIG

THE
HOUSEHOLDER'S
GUIDE TO
PLUMBING

STANLEY PAUL, LONDON

Stanley Paul and Company Ltd
3 Fitzroy Square, London W 1

London Melbourne Sydney Auckland
Wellington Johannesburg Cape Town
and agencies throughout the world

First published 1974
© James M. Haig 1961, 1973
Drawings © Stanley Paul & Company Ltd 1973

Set in Monotype Imprint
Made and printed in Great Britain by
William Clowes & Sons, Limited
London, Beccles and Colchester

ISBN 0 09 118430 4 (cased)
118431 2 (paper)

Contents

Acknowledgements

The author acknowledges with thanks the help he has received from the Copper, Lead and Zinc Development Associations, the Electrical Association, British Gas Corporation, Marley Plumbing Limited, Wednesbury Tube Company, Le Bas Tube Company Limited and Barking Brassware Company Limited, in the compilation of this book.

Foreword

This book is intended to help householders to acquire a sound knowledge of the functioning of the plumbing and central heating installations in their homes and enable them to undertake minor repairs and maintenance work. Every householder has a responsibility to his family and the community in being able to control the water and gas services within his home if only because of the safety factors involved. Apart from this he should know that inspection and maintenance can prevent deterioration which could lead to costly repairs and replacements.

The Householder's Guide to Plumbing is also aimed at the potential houseowner; knowing what to look for is all important as so many plumbing faults and inconsistencies are either hidden or virtually inaccessible. Thus anyone intending to purchase a new home should pay particular attention to the arrangement of pipework and the provisioning and positioning of stopvalves, and before making a final acceptance of the property, should closely inspect the surfaces of the bath, washbasin, wc pan and kitchen sink.

The materials and appliances used for plumbing and central heating and the skilled labour required to instal them are very costly. The extent and complexity of plumbing and heating have also increased with the introduction of more sophisticated appliances and accessories and by the improved standards of living enjoyed by everyone. Particular attention has been given to the increasing use of plastics in plumbing and the development of microbore copper tubes in central heating.

There is much new information about plumbing and heating

in this book which is completely up-to-date and metricised; *The Householder's Guide to Plumbing* will prove to be invaluable for apprentices and craftsmen as well as the serious do-it-yourself enthusiast.

Torbay, Devon   JAMES M. HAIG

1 | Cold Water supply explained

The Stopvalve

The plumbing system of a house begins at the stopvalve on the service pipe connecting with the town water main under the road. The stopvalve is the vital keypoint of the water supply to the house. Opened, it admits water to the plumbing system. When closed it isolates the house from the water main. The importance of this control point cannot be over-emphasized when explaining the plumbing system of a house to a householder. In an emergency such as a burst pipe, the speedy operation of the stopvalve could prevent the house from being flooded.

The stopvalve must be accessible. In older-type houses it might be found anywhere—under the pavement outside the house, beneath the path leading to the front door, or it might be in the front garden buried under two feet of earth! If it is in the cellar, unless the householder takes the necessary precautions he may find his path to the stopvalve barred by a mountain of coal—a formidable obstacle to a man in a hurry when a pipe has burst.

In more modern property one might expect to find the stopvalve in a box or pit (or maybe encased by a stoneware drainpipe) between the front gate and the front door. Wherever it is it should be located, made accessible and put in working order. There should be a hinged cover over the stopvalve and when this is opened it will probably be found that by stretching-out full length on the ground, and thrusting an arm down into the depths beneath the cover, it will be possible to touch the stopvalve with the tips of the fingers but not operate it. This is frustrating of course, but the householder should be consoled by the fact that the stopvalve is sufficiently below the ground to be protected from frost. Acrobatic contortions can be avoided by using a simple turnkey which can be made from wood or metal. Two types are illustrated in Fig. 1. The turnkey should be readily at hand at all times of the year, having mind to its importance in an emergency.

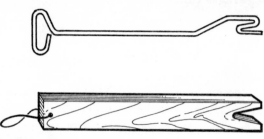

Fig. 1   Simple turnkeys

It is important for the householder to know that the stopvalve closes in a clockwise direction and that great pressure is not required to shut-off the water. The hinged flap of the cover should be kept clean and oiled occasionally. In an emergency the householder will not want to waste time prising open the flap.

STOPVALVES

Most Bye-laws require that:

'Every person who shall lay or use any service pipe shall permit the undertakers to fit thereon a stopvalve enclosed in a covered box or pit of such size as may be reasonably necessary and placed in a position as the undertakers deem most convenient.

Provided that a stopvalve in private premises shall be placed as near as reasonably practicable to the street from which the service pipe enters those premises.'

This means in effect that the water undertaking provides a connection to its water main and installs the service pipe to a convenient point and fits a stopvalve. From there the plumber continues the service pipe into the house.

The correct position of the stopvalve is illustrated in Fig. 2.

THE SERVICE PIPE INTO THE HOUSE

The service pipe from the house side of the stopvalve should continue at 0·750 m below the surface of the ground until it enters the premises. It is necessary to mention that certain soil conditions cause corrosion of metal pipes. Wet ashes, clinker, red marl clay, wet decomposing matter, wet ironstone have a more or less harmful effect on all metals. Where serious corrosion occurs it is usually due to a combination of poor drainage, high sulphate and/or chloride content of the ground, a prevailing moderate or heavy rainfall on earth of considerable moisture-retaining capacity.

Where corrosive conditions exist it is advisable to afford some protection to the service pipe. The most simple method is to paint

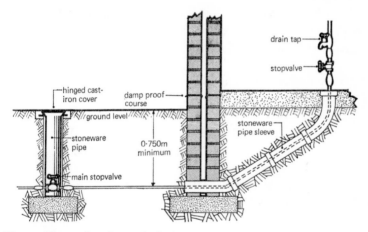

Fig. 2   The service pipe to the house

the pipe with bitumen, a material both suitable and easy to apply. Alternatively, the pipe can be surrounded to a distance of about 150 mm all round with limestone chippings which have the effect of neutralizing the acidity of the soil.

It has been common practice in the past for the plumber to take the service pipe into the house at a point adjacent to the kitchen sink. This may appear to be a sensible thing to do, considering that a branch is taken from the pipe to serve the cold water tap over the kitchen sink. Actually, it is bad practice, because no water pipe should be fixed in a position where it can be affected by frost. For this reason pipes should be fixed wherever possible to an inner partition wall, preferably in the warmest part of the kitchen. In Fig. 2 it will be seen that the service pipe is taken through a stoneware drain pipe and emerges well away from the perimeter wall.

Service pipes should not be embedded in concrete where this can be avoided. If they must be embedded or be in contact with concrete or cement they should be wrapped with waterproof building paper at the points of contact to allow free movement of the pipe and to prevent the metal from being in direct contact with cement.

It is advisable to slightly 'snake' the service pipe in the trench from the stopvalve to the house. This will provide length to allow for any minor subsidence in the soil.

STOPVALVE INSIDE THE HOUSE

The Bye-law states '. . . every service pipe supplying water to any building shall be fitted with a stopvalve inside, and as near as practicable to the point of entry of such pipe into the building'.

There are hundreds of thousands of houses without a stopvalve on the service pipe within the house. To the owners of such houses the key point of the cold water system remains the stopvalve outside. They are not bound to have a stopvalve fitted inside but the advantages are obvious. The stopvalve is readily accessible and for convenience it can be shut down at night in frosty weather.

It is a sound plan to fit a draincock as close as possible to the internal stopvalve to enable the service pipe to be turned off and drained. This should be a routine precaution during a spell of frosty weather.

A combination stopvalve and draincock is available from suppliers of plumbers' brassware.

THE RISING MAIN

The service pipe within the house is usually referred to by plumbers as the rising main. This is because it is the pipe conveying mains water, and it rises up through the house to feed the storage cistern in the roof space.

The rising main provides drinking water and, in some areas, cold water to the bath, washbasin and w.c. cistern. The local Bye-laws should be consulted because many water undertakings do not permit direct connection of sanitary and ablutionary fitments with main water.

The rising main should be fixed to an internal partition wall, but in many houses it will be found on the inside of the perimeter wall of the kitchen and bathroom, and in some cases will be close to the ventilator in the bathroom or w.c. and right in the line of icy draughts in wintertime.

The wise householder will trace the run of his rising main and take steps to ensure that it is protected from frost. Advice on this subject is given in the section of this book dealing with frost protection.

The Storage Cistern

The question is often posed 'why must we have a tank in the roof when everything could be supplied from the main?'

First, the difference between a tank and a cistern must be made clear. Far too many plumbers call a cistern a tank and this is both confusing and incorrect.

A *cistern* is a container for water which is under atmospheric pressure (i.e. an open top). A *storage cistern* is any cistern other than a flushing cistern. A *feed cistern* is for supplying cold water to a hot water apparatus.

A *tank* is a closed container for water under more than atmospheric pressure. The term is used in household plumbing for the hot water tank (or cylinder).

The container in the roof space of a house is a *storage cistern* and it has a threefold purpose: (i) It provides a reserve of water if for any reason the main supply is cut off. (ii) It limits the pressure of water on pipes and fittings within the house thus reducing noises in the pipes, wastage of water, and enabling pipes of a lighter weight (and less costly) to be used. (iii) It reduces the maximum rate of demand on the company's mains supply.

Further to these points, everyone should know that water undertakers must take the utmost precautions to ensure that the main water supply shall not become contaminated. It is for this reason that some undertakings do not permit mains water to be connected direct to w.c. flushing cisterns, baths, washbasins or to certain types of mixing valves. They fear the possibility of water contamination. There are in fact recorded cases of mains water becoming contaminated by what is technically known as 'back-siphonage', or in simple terms, fouled water being drawn back into the main supply. It is the duty of every householder to co-operate with the water undertakings in preserving the purity of mains water.

THE POSITION OF THE STORAGE CISTERN

The customary practice is to place the storage cistern in the roof space. There are two points in favour of this: (i) The roof space is the highest part of the house and a cistern fixed there will ensure a good pressure of water at the taps below. This is of particular importance if a shower is to be used in the bathroom. (ii) A cistern can be rather noisy when it is refilling and in the roof space it is more or less out of hearing—and certainly out of sight.

There is an increasing tendency to place the cistern as high as possible but not actually in the roof space. It can be fixed in a cupboard on the landing directly above the hot water storage tank. The 'head of water' which governs pressure will be reduced, but it will scarcely affect the supply of water at the various taps in the house.

If it is decided to fix the cistern in a cupboard, it should be as high as possible but with sufficient space left between the top and the ceiling to permit the cistern to be inspected and cleaned, and for repairs to be carried out on the ball valve when necessary. The cistern should be supported very firmly because a full cistern of water is very heavy indeed.

If the cistern is placed in the roof space it must be protected against frost. If the roof is not close boarded and insulated it can be the coldest place in the house and truly arctic conditions may prevail in the winter, with icy blasts sweeping under the tiles or through the eaves. If coal fires are used—or any solid fuel for that matter—the cistern can be sited adjacent to the chimney breast, as this can be quite warm. The cistern should be insulated and be fitted with a cover. An outer casing of wood is built around the cistern leaving a space of at least 50 mm to be filled with a non-conducting material, i.e. granulated cork, sawdust or one of the proprietary brands of insulating materials. The top of the cistern should also be insulated by providing a cover lined with hair felt and fixed 50 mm clear above the dust cover. Provision must be made for adequate ventilation inside the protective cover.

The cistern should be carried on wood bearers but the weight should not be borne directly by the ceiling joists.

If the cistern is fixed in a warm cupboard it will not require an insulated casing but it should have a dust cover. The possibility of condensation must be considered and it might be necessary to provide a metal drip tray.

CAPACITY OF THE STORAGE CISTERN
It is not necessary to lay down any hard and fast rules about the size of the storage cistern except to stress that the water regulations require that they shall conform to the minimum capacity requirements. The local water undertaking should be consulted before a decision is made.

The water requirements of individuals and families differ considerably but it is known that the average daily consumption per head of the population increases yearly and is now probably in the region of 160 litres. This does not mean that these figures should form the basis for calculating the storage cistern capacity for a family, because some members of the household may draw much of their water requirements from sources outside the home such as at the place of work, public buildings and the homes of friends.

The storage cistern refills automatically through the ball valve—when water is drawn and it is unlikely that in any home that the storage could become exhausted, unless for some reason the main supply was seriously reduced or cut off altogether. There is the odd occasion when the ball valve gets jammed, preventing the incoming supply to enter the cistern but this is very rare indeed.

A cistern with a capacity of from 350 to 500 litres would be sufficient for the average 3-bedroomed house but reference to the water regulations could settle the point.

THE REGULATIONS

Although the water regulations may differ from place to place the following requirements will always apply:

(a) The cistern shall be fitted with an efficient warning pipe and with no other overflow pipe.

(b) The internal diameter of the warning pipe shall be greater than the internal diameter of the inlet pipe and in no case less than 22 mm.

(c) The overflowing level of the warning pipe shall be set

(i) below the top edge of the cistern at a distance of not less than twice the diameter of the warning pipe and,

(ii) above the water-line at a distance of not less than 28 mm or not less than the internal diameter of the warning pipe whichever is the greater.

The provision of protection against frost and a well-fitting but not airtight cover is also required by the regulations.

MATERIALS FOR CISTERNS

The majority of cisterns installed in dwelling houses all over the country are manufactured from galvanized iron. These cisterns give excellent trouble free service for 25 years and more providing they are properly installed and protected. They are even better suited for hard water districts when a protective coat of lime quickly forms on the internal surfaces. In very soft water areas the effective life of the cistern will be less and an asbestos, glass fibre or plastics cistern would be advisable.

In recent years the development of plastics cisterns has been rapid and these have many advantages over the other forms.

Polypropylene cisterns have a greater rigidity than those made from polythene but this advantage is not so apparent if the cistern is to be used in an existing house, because it cannot be folded to permit its passage through a restricted trap door into the roof space. This factor is not important of course in new buildings when the cistern can be placed in position before the ceiling or trap door are completed.

Plastics cisterns are made in various sizes all to conform to regulations. They may be rectangular or circular in shape and are very light and easy to handle. They are unaffected by any type of water and of course there are no problems of electrolytic action.

The glass fibre polyester resin cisterns are also gaining popularity. They are non-toxic, stain resistant and have excellent chemical insulation properties.

It is very important that the manufacturer's instructions be followed when installing plastics cisterns. There have been failures due to wrongful use and from incorrect installation. This applies particularly to cisterns being used to feed hot water systems. Under certain conditions, some plastics are affected by excessive heat such as very hot water. The plumber is advised to acquaint himself with the performance characteristics of plastics cisterns and order the right one for the job in hand.

All things being equal, there are distinct advantages to be gained by installing a suitable plastics cistern.

DISTRIBUTION PIPES

Distributing pipes convey water from the storage cistern to the various fitments in the house. The definition in the Bye-laws is: 'any pipe conveying water supplied by the undertakers from a storage cistern or from a hot water apparatus supplied from a feed cistern and under pressure from such cistern.'

The distributing pipe system calls for careful design and correct installation technique. The designer—and the plumber—must consider pipe sizing, avoidance of air-locks, noise transmission, contamination of mains water, protection against frost, corrosion and damage, and of course economy in the use of labour and materials. Unfortunately, the tendency is to take the pipes on the shortest route from the storage cistern to the bathroom, regardless of the fact that it might not be the best route. This is done either from ignorance of the correct principles or to cut down costs—perhaps both.

The protection of pipes required in the Bye-laws includes the avoidance of water contamination. It is important that the householder should know something about this if he is ever tempted to effect alterations to the plumbing system of his house. There must never be any cross connection between a pipe carrying mains water and any pipe or fitting containing water that is impure or liable to contamination in any way.

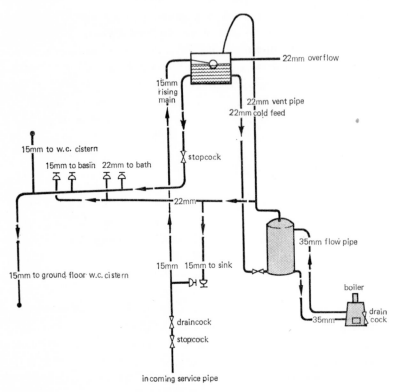

Fig. 3   Layout of typical household cold and hot water systems

The hazard of water pollution within a plumbing system is a very serious one and is dealt with more fully in the next chapter.

The householder should trace the run of the distributing pipes in his house and identify their purpose. It is customary for one pipe to be taken from the storage cistern to supply the cold water to the bath, washbasin and w.c. cistern—and any other appliances that may be installed. A separate pipe from the storage cistern supplies cold water to the hot water system and this is known as the cold feed pipe. It is not a distributing pipe in the accepted sense of the term.

A distributing pipe should be controlled by a stopvalve as near as possible to the cistern but in a position where it is easily accessible to the householder. If there is no stopvalve on the pipe then one should be fixed as soon as possible—it might be the means of preventing flooding in the event of a burst pipe.

In Fig. 3, the distributing pipes, hot water installation and rising mains are shown in diagrammatical form.

2 | Cold Water Installation

Preliminary Considerations

When water supply is obtained from the mains, the water undertaking's Bye-laws must be observed, so they should be studied before any work is commenced. The plumber, or whoever is responsible for the installation, must submit details of the proposed work for approval by the water undertaking.

Some undertakings require a consumer to take the supply—with the exception of drinking water—through a storage cistern. Others do not ask for a storage cistern at all.

Water undertakings provide printed forms for use by the plumber. These include:

(a) Application for a supply of water.

(b) Request to lay a communication (service) pipe.

(c) Notices that whole or part of the service is complete and ready for inspection by the undertaking.

Form filling and submission should be completed in good time in order to prevent delays in obtaining approval for the work and the supply of water to the premises.

There are occasions when the undertaking may require the supply to be taken through a meter, in which case an agreement will have to be completed by the consumer.

It is important to know that the householder is responsible for any alterations or additions made to the water supply in his house. If work has been installed by a plumber who has not previously notified the water undertaking of what he intended to do and when subsequently inspected it is found not to conform to the undertaking's Bye-laws it is the householder who will have to foot the bill for such alterations as may be required. The householder should therefore ensure that his plumber has complied with the requirements before allowing him to do the work.

LAYING THE SERVICE PIPE

It is usual for the water undertaking to drill the main and lay the service—or, as it is often called, the communication—pipe, to the stopvalve. The owner of the building pays for this service. When the undertaking permits the plumber to lay the pipe from the main, the actual connection of the ferrule to the main is made by the undertaking, also at the building owner's expense. When the plumber lays the communication pipe from the main he should have it inspected by the undertaking before filling-in the trench.

When a house is being built in such a position that it may be necessary to lay a new main or extend an existing main, full details of the house and site should be submitted to the water undertaking as early as possible. The cost of laying or extending the main will be borne by the water undertaking providing the annual income in water rates from the new services to be taken from the mains will be sufficient to reach a prescribed fraction (usually one-eighth) of the total cost. The building owner should be quite clear about his position in this respect well beforehand.

Design Considerations

PROTECTION AGAINST CONTAMINATION

The water undertakings of this country do everything within their power to ensure that the supply of water at the household tap is pure and satisfactory for drinking and culinary purposes. It is probable that the water supply in Britain is as good as any in the world. It is of the utmost importance, therefore, that it should not be liable to contamination from any source. There must be no interconnection or cross-connection whatsoever between a pipe or fitting for containing or conveying wholesome water and a pipe or fitting containing impure water, water liable to contamination or of uncertain quality, or water that has been used for any purpose. The provision of reflux or non-return valves is not a permissible substitute for complete absence of connection.

The pipe work of the house must be so designed that there is no possibility of backflow towards the source of supply from any cistern or appliance, whether by siphonage or otherwise. All pipework must be made completely watertight and must not be laid through any sewer or drain or manhole nor in ground contaminated by sewage.

Every water inlet to a fixed bath or washbasin must be distinct from, and unconnected with, the outlet. Draw-off taps or ball valves discharging into cisterns or appliances must be fixed so that the outlet of the tap or valve cannot be submerged when the water in the cistern or appliance is at overflowing level. This precaution is to avoid possible contamination by backflow or back-siphonage into the main water supply.

It is essential that only mixing valves and hot and cold water tap assemblies shall be of the type approved by the water undertaking. Attachments fixed to taps or outlets should never be left in such a position that back siphonage of polluted water into the supply system can occur.

PIPE SIZING AND DISCHARGE RATES

Information for determining the size of a pipe for any given purpose is based on the rate of discharge required, the length of the pipe, the head available for loss by friction in that length and the roughness of the internal surface of the piping. This information is available to the plumber in the form of tables, formulae and diagrams, for use in designing water supply. It is necessary to make due allowance to provide against the loss of discharging capacity due to the internal incrustation of the pipes in the course of time.

To keep piping down to a minimum size with a consequent reduction in the cost of installation, the designer must give consideration to layout, and see to it that changes in diameter and direction are gradual rather than abrupt to avoid loss of head. All bends in pipes should be made so as not to diminish materially or alter their cross-sections. The pipes should be as smooth as possible internally, and the methods of jointing be such as to avoid internal roughness and projections at the joints. It might be mentioned here that the effective diameter of a pipe is reduced and severe friction set up if material used for jointing pipes is applied in such a manner that it adheres to the internal surface of the pipe or fitting.

CHOICE OF MATERIALS FOR PIPING

In choosing the material of the piping and fittings, apart from the character of the water, there are the considerations of cost, appearance, personal preferences and of course the Bye-laws. The merits of lead, copper, iron and plastic pipes are dealt with in another section of the Guide, but it will be as well to mention at this point important facts which must not be overlooked when a final choice is being made.

Lead piping must not be used to convey water so soft in nature that it is plumbo solvent, which means taking lead into solution. There would be a danger of lead poisoning. Copper can be dissolved by certain waters, and although water containing a small amount of copper may be quite wholesome, it can produce green stains, particularly in contact with soap. Iron piping is liable to severe corrosion by some waters and internal incrustation may be formed which in the course of time can entirely choke pipes of small bore.

ELECTROLYTIC ACTION

It must be mentioned that electrolytic action can be set up by the contact of certain dissimilar metals and this may result in corrosion. In particular, the use of copper pipes with galvanized iron tanks or cylinders could cause accelerated corrosion to the vessels due to copper being taken into solution and being deposited on the surface of the galvanized iron. Less frequently, similar trouble may be experienced with galvanized iron cisterns.

It is advisable to use copper hot water tanks or cylinders when copper piping is used and the galvanized storage cistern should be painted inside with a bituminous composition.

MINIMUM STRENGTH OF PIPES

The Bye-laws of the water undertakings specify the minimum strength of piping required for service pipes and distributing pipes. It is necessary to comply with Bye-laws in every case.

AVOIDANCE OF AIRLOCKS AND NOISE TRANSMISSION

The installation of pipework is not just a matter of running a pipe to or from a storage cistern by the shortest route. This slipshod attitude has caused untold damage, inconvenience, frustration and unnecessary expenditure on maintenance and repairs.

Services should be so designed and installed to avoid air-locks, and ensure that all pipes in the house can be completely emptied of water to facilitate repairs and as a precaution if the building is to be left unheated in frosty weather. There should be draw-off or drain taps at the lowest points, from which the piping should rise continuously to draw-off taps, ball valves, cisterns or vents at the highest points.

To avoid unnecessary noise in plumbing, high velocity of water in pipes should be avoided and easy bends should be used to permit the smooth passage of water. All brackets and clips should be insulated from the piping by suitable pads, particularly if the pipes pass through living-rooms or bedrooms.

The rush of water into w.c. cisterns fed from the main often gives rise to noise transmission. It is advisable to fit a 'silencer' pipe which in effect is a copper tube soldered or screwed to the outlet of the valve in the cistern to convey the incoming water to the bottom of the cistern thus reducing the noise. If this pipe is used, holes must be provided in the pipe or body of the valve to prevent the possibility of siphonage back into the main. These holes must be above the overflowing level of the cistern.

A nuisance in any plumbing system is 'water hammer'. When a column of water in motion is suddenly stopped by a tap being turned off quickly, a noise which resembles a sharp blow with a hammer is heard in the pipes. This is caused by the moving water exerting its force against the wall of the pipe. Water hammer by creating shock waves can cause pipes to burst. A pipe conveying water is continually under stress and the higher the pressure the greater the strain. While this pressure remains constant, and of course is within the bursting limit of the pipe, then little strain is imposed on the pipe; but when the pressure is permitted to

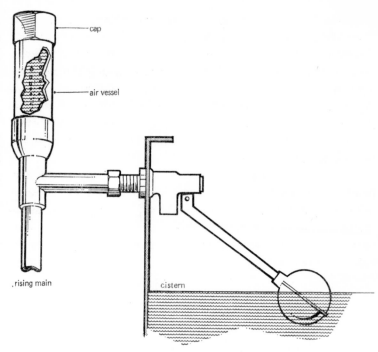

Fig. 4   Preventing 'water hammer'

fluctuate wildly over very wide limits, then an expansion and contraction of the pipe diameter will result. Although this movement is of course microscopic its continued influence is accumulative and may result in permanent deformation of the pipe and eventual bursting. Although it is characteristic that the noise is sharp—like a hammer blow—the hum of a ball valve as it vibrates in a storage cistern also indicates that undue stresses are prevailing in the supply line. One method of combating water hammer at the ball valve of the storage cistern is to install an air chamber (see Fig. 4). An air chamber is formed by a pipe of larger diameter than the service pipe and is fixed in an upright position as shown. As it may have to withstand considerable pressure the air chamber must be strongly constructed and must be airtight.

When the water supply is turned on, air in the chamber is

compressed and when a tap is opened the pressure on the air is reduced, and the air is able to expand. When a tap is suddenly closed, instead of the pipe bearing the shock of the water hammer, the air is compressed by the blow and gently expands and contracts until the pressure of the compressed air equals the pressure of the water. When air chambers are installed the air has to be periodically recharged. This is done by turning off the water supply, draining the pipes, and allowing the air into the chamber by opening a tap nearby.

Ball valves sometimes cause water hammer, due to the float being raised and lowered by waves on the surface of the water in the cistern. One remedy is to solder a piece of sheet copper to the bottom of the ball in the form of a flat fin. The fin remains about one inch below the surface of the water and prevents the ball from oscillating.

PLANNING THE PIPE RUNS

All pipes should be so placed that they will not be exposed to accidental damage, and fixed in such positions as to facilitate cleaning and avoid accumulations of dirt. Pipework should be accessible for inspection, replacement and repair. Nobody likes to see pipes and if they can be hidden away so much the better. Providing there is sufficient space to work with the normal tools the plumber can usually arrange his pipes to run through, or adjacent to, cupboards or in recesses. Where pipes are run under floorboards the boards should be fixed with screws to facilitate removal at any time.

Pipes should not be buried in walls or solid floors. There is a tendency to provide ducts or chases for pipework in modern homes. These should be properly constructed to prevent the possible entry of vermin.

If it is necessary for a pipe to run in a wood floor it should, wherever possible, be parallel with the joists. Pipes passing through walls or floors should be sleeved to allow freedom for expansion and contraction and other movement.

Installation Precautions

Before any pipe is used for installation work care must be taken to ensure that it is the correct pipe for the job. The pipe must conform to the Bye-laws with regard to quality and weight.

The pipe should be inspected to see that it is clean internally, and free from particles of sand or soil, metal filings or chips, which, apart from causing obstructions, might well lead to failure by corrosion.

In jointing pipes all internal burrs must be removed and care taken to prevent any jointing material entering the pipes for fear of causing obstruction, corrosion or giving rise to water contamination.

The joints should be cleaned off externally as should any marks made by tools. The screws of holder-bats or other type of pipe fixing should be checked for tightness.

If the sleeves are to be used where the pipes pass through walls they must be slipped over the pipe before it is jointed.

No work should be built-in until it has been fully tested. When testing, care must be taken to eliminate all air from the pipes.

3 | Hot Water Supply Explained

A piped hot water supply is regarded as essential in every home. There are of course still far too many homes without this modern convenience, but to build a house today without installing a hot water system of some kind would be unthinkable.

There is more to it than just deciding that a hot water system should be installed. The system must meet all the hot water requirements of the household, operate efficiently with the minimum attention and not be too expensive to run. For these reasons a great deal of thought must be given to selection, design and installation.

First Considerations

The basic requirement is to provide hot water to the kitchen sink, the bath and washbasin. In large houses there may be washbasins in the bedrooms and downstairs cloakroom and perhaps a second bathroom. Probably the first decision to make is what type of fuel shall be used for heating the water. There are four main fuels, namely, solid fuel, gas, electricity and oil. The decision to use one of these fuels must inevitably be influenced by general considerations as well as preference. How is the house to be heated? That is possibly the first question the plumber will ask the householder. It is obvious that if the fuel used for heating the house can be utilized to heat the water as well this is an economic proposition, hence the great popularity in this country at one time of the boiler at the back of the living-room fire. In fact, although hot water and heating installations in the home have today become popular topics and have caused the suppliers of fuels and the manufacturers of appliances to seek control of the markets through extensive and costly advertising campaigns, there is still something to commend the simple but properly installed domestic hot water system comprising a boiler at the back of the fire or behind a purpose built gas-fire, and a tank or cylinder in the linen cupboard. In the winter, with the living-room fire alight all day and every day to heat the room, hot water costs very little. In the summer an electric immersion heater in the storage vessel will provide hot water for most purposes at a reasonable cost.

There is a wide and fascinating choice for the householder today and in the following pages the field of hot water supply is dealt with.

HOT WATER REQUIREMENTS
Hot water is required for the following purposes:

Baths
Large supply at infrequent intervals day or night with the possibility of consecutive baths.

Washbasin
Small supplies at infrequent intervals morning and night.

Kitchen Sink
Moderate supplies at frequent intervals mainly during the day.

Cooking
Small supplies of very hot water during the day.

Clothes Washing
Large supplies of hot water on certain days only and moderate supplies for washing 'smalls' at irregular intervals.

Sundries
Small supplies of very hot water to be available day or night for cleaning, illness, hot water bottles, etc.

From the foregoing it would seem that there must be an adequate storage of hot water as well as means of obtaining quantities of very hot water immediately for many purposes, including consumption.

The problem of small supplies fit for human consumption and for filling hot water bottles, etc., can be disposed of by the choice of the traditional kettle to be heated by gas or electricity—or to be on the hob—or the installation of a small 'over-the-sink' gas or electric appliance which will provide small quantities of boiling water very quickly.

PLANNING

In planning a hot water system a qualified plumber will work on the basis that the heating appliance must occupy the minimum of floor space, as must also the space for the storage vessel and fuel storage. The system selected must permit some latitude in estimating hot water requirements and allow flexibility in the general planning of the house. The plumbing work must be simple and the installation should be adaptable to conversion and extension.

After the planning stage, the next step is to consider the convenience of the system. It must be capable of maintaining constant supplies day and night with a minimum of attention. There should be provision for the changing requirements of the family and for individual preferences. The hot water must be delivered at the taps in sufficient volume and at a controlled temperature. The main appliance should provide space heating in the winter, avoid overheating the house in summer and be of good appearance.

Some thought must be given to labour saving and there should be cleanliness in working and fuel provision. As previously stated, it should require the minimum attendance time in operating. Maintenance requirements should be very little as should flue cleaning and the cleaning of the apparatus itself.

Finally, the apparatus must give the greatest efficiency at the lowest possible running cost.

The Gravity System of Hot Water Supply

HEAD OF WATER

The majority of domestic hot water systems in the homes in the UK are of the gravity type. In simple terms, the motive power to circulate the hot water is derived from the cold water storage cistern situated in the roof or at some other high point in the house.

The pressure of water at any point in the system is caused by the vertical column of water between that point and the level of water in the cold water cistern. The higher the column of water the greater the pressure. We have now adopted SI units for plumbing in the UK and the symbols lb/sq in or p.s.i. for 'pounds per square inch' have been replaced by Newtons per square metre or N/m^2. In cases of low pressure the symbol is mbar, which means millibar. So if a tap is supplied with water under a head of 3 metres the pressure at the tap is equal to 3 cubic metres or 3,000 kg of water exerting downward force or pressure. The pressure on the tap is defined as $29 \cdot 43$ kN/m^2.

The greater the head at the tap, the greater will be the flow of water when the tap is opened. The flow of water from the tap at the washbasin in the bathroom will be less than that from the tap over the kitchen sink on the ground floor which has a greater head of water.

More water will flow from a large tap than from a small one because the large tap offers less resistance to the flow of water than the small one. The same applies to the pipings and fittings leading to the tap. The actual flow of water at the tap thus depends upon the head of water and the resistance of the pipes and fittings connecting that tap to the cold water cistern.

The resistance of a length of pipe or of a pipe fitting is not a constant amount. In fact, the resistance increases as the flow of water increases, so that for the same pipe run a larger flow will mean increased resistance. Conversely, a pipe run of increased resistance will give a smaller flow for the same head.

The resistance of a pipe is expressed in 'loss of head per metre run of pipe' and, to avoid confusion, the resistance of fittings and of the tap itself is considered as being equivalent to many metres run of piping of the same size.

CIRCULATION

We have dealt with the flow of water when a tap is opened, but there is another type of flow of importance in hot water installation, known as 'circulation'. In this case the water does not flow out of the system but merely flows or circulates round the circuit of piping. There must be a 'head' of water to cause circulation and it is this head and the resistance of the pipes and fittings making the circuit that determines the rate of circulation.

Circulation is an essential feature of hot water systems and it is desirable that the householder should have some knowledge of the primary principles.

It is so often said that hot water rises, but although this may be an easy and convenient way of describing circulation, it is not strictly true. It is the cold water that provides the motive force in hot water circulation. Water particles expand when they are heated and become larger than the cooler particles. As the heated particles do not increase in weight they become, bulk for bulk, lighter than the others. The heated particles of water cannot rise on their own account but are pushed upwards by the heavier, colder particles. This principle is applied in hot water systems for conveying the heated water from the boiler to the hot storage vessel.

In Fig. 5 imagine that the water in both the boiler and storage vessel is cold. It will be quickly realized that circulation cannot occur because the two columns of water AB (consisting of the flow pipe AC and the boiler itself CB) and DG (consisting of the vessel DE and the return pipe EG) are at the same temperature, have the same weight and thus balance each other.

When heat is applied to the water in the boiler it becomes lighter than the water in the corresponding length FG of the return pipe so that on the whole column DG is heavier than the column AG. The water in the heavier column falls and forces the heated water from the boiler up the flow pipe AC and thus circulation

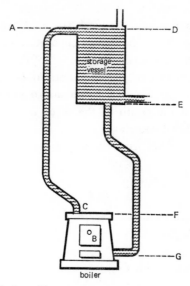

Fig. 5   The circulation of hot water

commences. The circulation will continue until both columns are at the same temperature.

In actual fact, so long as the fire in the boiler burns normally, circulation will go on because heat will be continually lost from the surface of the pipes and the storage vessel and the water in the return pipe will always be lower in temperature than that in the flow pipe.

It will be seen that the flow and return pipes are connected to the top and the bottom respectively of the boiler. If they were both taken from the top of the boiler it would be uncertain as to which pipe became the flow and which the return. If both pipes were taken from the bottom of the boiler, no circulation would take place as the heating of the boiler would not put the two columns out of balance.

If both flow and return pipes were taken to the top of the hot water storage vessel, the hot water would circulate across the top of the vessel and the lower part would remain cold. If both flow and return pipes were taken to the bottom of the storage vessel the whole of the contents would be ultimately heated, but the entering hot water would mix with the cold water in the vessel and a gradual heating of the whole contents would take place.

When the flow pipe is taken to the top of the hot water storage vessel and the return pipe from the bottom, as in Fig. 5, the hot water from the boiler will tend to remain in a layer on top of the colder water and the depth of the layer will increase until the whole vessel is filled with hot water. The effect is that hot water is available for draw off from the top of the vessel in the shortest possible time.

4 | Hot Water Installation

The basic problem in any domestic hot water installation is to convert the incoming supply of cold water into a constant supply of hot water at the kitchen sink, bath and washbasin—and to any additional points so required.

The planning stage has already been discussed and in this chapter a typical installation will be discussed, assuming that there will be a combination of a boiler, and an electric immersion heater in the hot water storage vessel. There are a great many variations of this combination but only the basic principles will be explained. The installation will be of the gravity type. An accelerated system combined with space heating by hot water is dealt with in the chapter on 'Smallbore Heating'. Electric water heaters and gas water heaters are also dealt with separately.

TYPE OF BOILER

The type of boiler used has but little effect upon the design of the system. It may be an independent boiler or a back boiler in an open fire, gasfire, stove or range, but the only difference between these various alternatives from the design point of view is the position of the boiler. In the case of a back boiler in an open fire, stove or gas fire, it will usually be in the living-room while in the case of an independent boiler or a back boiler in a range it will usually be in the kitchen. In either case the position of the boiler will be determined by the planning and lay-out of the house and it will not normally be possible to alter its position to suit the lay-out of the hot water system. The boiler becomes the focal point of a combined installation and the design must start there.

A golden rule for any combined installation is that it should be designed for the highest possible efficiency and economy when using electricity only. This will reduce the running cost to a minimum when electricity is being used and as electricity is normally used in the summer it will avoid unwanted heat in the house at times when it is least welcome.

High efficiency from electric power can be obtained without interfering in any way with satisfactory performance when run on other fuels.

This improved performance may give rise to problems and will almost certainly demand pipework layouts that differ from the conventional.

There is a world of difference between designing an installation for a new house where there is a degree of freedom in design and converting to combined operation an existing system where the layout is governed by its apparatus and piping already installed.

Because it would be impossible to deal separately with the conversion of the unlimited variety of installations to be seen in homes all over the UK, we will confine our guidelines to the system in a new house.

THE POSITION OF THE BOILER
The usual practice is to install the boiler and the storage vessel near each other in order to make the flow and return connections as short as possible and thus to reduce not only the cost of piping but also the heat losses from the piping. Where it is intended to use electricity for the water heating in the summer the need for this practice does not exist. The boiler will only be used in winter when the heat losses from the flow and return piping might be a welcome contribution towards heating the house. If the system is considered for water heating alone its efficiency would be very low indeed owing to the heat losses from the system and the fact that the minimum amount of fuel necessary to keep the fire alight produces a good deal more heat than is required to heat the amount of hot water used by a normal family. On the other hand, if the solid-fuel system is used as a combined water and space heating installation and all the heat losses contribute towards space heating, the efficiency is relatively high and there is some justification for

the theory that in such cases, the only loss of efficiency is due to the heat in the flue gases leaving the boiler chimney.

It will be appreciated that, although the flue gas will leave the boiler at a relatively high temperature, most of its heat will be lost to the walls of the chimney which in turn helps to warm the house.

FLOW AND RETURN PIPING

A long run of flow and return piping will be no drawback provided that the circulation between the boiler and the storage vessel is adequate. Adequate circulation between boiler and storage vessel is very important and if not provided for can give rise to trouble. If the circulation is sluggish, the boiler will have to be 'forced' in order to heat up the storage vessel in a reasonable space of time. Forcing the boiler means an extremely hot fire with excessive formation of clinker, burning of the fire bars and a loss of efficiency. In addition, it means high water temperatures which in hard water districts will lead to trouble from scale forming in the system.

There is a tendency to make flow and return pipes too small, and this is a far more likely cause of sluggish circulation than a long run of flow and return piping. It is quite common to make the pipes 28 mm in diameter, often even only 22 mm whereas in hard water districts nothing smaller than 35 mm should be used. A 28 mm pipe will scale up with alarming rapidity but the use of 35 mm defers the evil day to an extent out of all proportion to the difference in size and cost.

POSITION OF STORAGE VESSEL

The position of the storage vessel can be decided without being governed by the position of the boiler, provided it is possible to install flow and return piping between the two and that the vessel is at a higher level than the boiler.

If we consider the usual 'dead leg' pipe to the kitchen sink, the best place for the hot water storage vessel is between the boiler and the sink and as near as practicable to the latter. This will usually mean that it is positioned immediately below the ground floor ceiling and it must be so placed that it can be insulated to a thickness of three inches all round.

An alternative position for the storage vessel is in the linen cupboard and this is often adopted, the idea being to heat the linen cupboard by means of the storage vessel itself. If an immersion heater is fitted the vessel must be well insulated to prevent waste of electricity and the size of the linen cupboard should therefore be sufficiently large to allow a clear space of three inches all round and above the storage vessel. When the vessel has been insulated the housewife may think that there is not enough heat given off. Sometimes it is suggested that a section of the insulation should be made removable but this is not recommended because it will cause an appreciable increase in the electricity bill. The housewife will find through experience that the amount of heat escaping from a well-insulated storage vessel is quite sufficient to keep linen aired, because the flow of heat, although not great at any instant, is maintained day and night by electric heating under thermostatic control.

BACK CIRCULATION

A common method of connecting the flow and return pipes is for these to enter the side of the storage vessel at high and low levels respectively as in Fig. 6A. This arrangement in certain circumstances is unsatisfactory because contrary to the generally accepted view that hot water will not circulate downwards, it is possible for circulation of hot water through the boiler to take place when the immersion heater only is in use.

Assume that the storage vessel is full of hot water, having been heated up by the immersion heater, but that the rest of the system is cold. The two columns of water AC and DE are not in balance because although the two portions BC and EF are at the same temperature, the portions AB and DE are not, AB being hot and DE being cold. Consequently a circulation will be set up in the reverse direction to that taken when the boiler is in use.

However rapid the back circulation, the part DE will always be

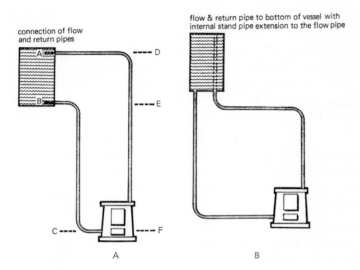

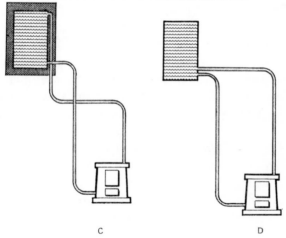

Fig. 6   Connection of flow and return pipes

cooler than AB because there will be a loss of heat from the horizontal length of pipe AD. In fact, the longer AD is the more rapid the circulation will be, other factors being the same. It is also true that the loss of heat from the circuit in general will mean that BC will be cooler than EF and this will oppose the back circulation. If the storage vessel is on the floor above the boiler the vertical distance is usually sufficient to prevent back circulation, but if the vertical distance is less than four feet, as it may be in a bungalow or flat, the circulation may be far from negligible.

In the interests of economy there should be no circulation at all. Even a sluggish circulation, one so sluggish that the boiler is barely perceptibly warmer than the air, will lead to quite a large bill for wasted electricity. The fitting of an isolating valve in the flow and return pipe would certainly stop the circulation but any such valve might be a source of danger when the boiler was in use and in any case experience has shown that the only valve the housewife can be relied on to use is one controlling a visible flow of water. Any valve installed to stop unwanted circulation would most likely be left open until an excessive bill for electricity acted as a belated reminder. The problem will be solved if the pipe DE is kept at the same temperature as AB and this can be done by taking both flow and return pipes to the bottom of the storage vessel and extending the flow pipe to within 50 mm of the top by means of an internal stand pipe as shown in Fig. 6B.

Another method is to run the flow pipe as near to the storage vessel as possible and to incorporate the pipe in the insulation of the storage vessel as in Fig. 6C. This will ensure that the flow pipe is kept at practically the same temperature as the storage vessel.

In cases where both flow and return pipes are taken into the side of the storage vessel at low level as in Fig. 6D the risk of back circulation is slight as the height of the out-of-balance columns is so small, but with this arrangement the boiler does not give hot water quickly at the top of the cylinder.

COLD WATER FEED PIPE

This pipe must be connected to the storage vessel at low level so that the incoming cold water will displace the hot water in the vessel without mixing with it. If mixing does occur, the full hot water content of the vessel will not be available for use, because when some of the hot water is drawn off, the vessel will be filled with a tepid mixture of hot and cold water instead of having a layer of hot water at the top with a layer of cold underneath.

One way of doing this is to take the cold feed pipe through the top of the storage vessel and continue it downwards by means of an inverted stand pipe inside the vessel terminating 25 mm or so above the bottom of the vessel as in Fig. 7A.

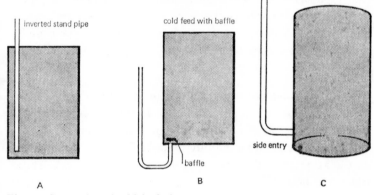

Fig. 7   *Connection of cold feed pipe*

This arrangement will prevent mixing of the incoming water with the hot water in the vessel, but as the internal stand pipe will be heated by contact with the hot water in the vessel, single-pipe circulation with consequent loss of heat will take place unless the pipe is run horizontally for a distance of about 450 mm immediately after leaving the top of the vessel.

If the pipe is taken through the bottom of the vessel a baffle will be necessary as in Fig. 7B, as otherwise the stream of cold water possibly entering at considerable velocity when there is a heavy rate of draw-off will be forced in the form of a jet to the top of the vessel and will mix with the hot water.

A better arrangement is to take the cold feed into the side of the vessel at low level. This is the standard connection to a cylinder as shown in Fig. 7C. The level of the cold feed connection should not be below the top of the domed bottom, otherwise cold water entering quickly would be deflected upwards by the slope of the dome and cause undue mixing.

There is a general tendency for cold feed pipes to be too small in diameter. Taking a flow figure of 36 litres/min, the velocity of the water in a 15 mm pipe is about 3·048 m/sec, in a 22 mm pipe 1·828 m/sec, in a 28 mm pipe 1·0972 m/sec, and in a 35 mm pipe 0·6400 m/sec, and these figures show clearly how with anything less than 28 mm trouble is to be expected. Obviously, the cold feed pipe should not be smaller than the main draw-off pipe as the flow of water will be the same in both pipes. One effect of too small a cold feed pipe is a severe reduction in, or complete cessation of, flow from the bathroom taps when the sink tap is in use.

VENT PIPE

A vent pipe must be taken from the top of the storage vessel and discharged above the cold feed cistern. Its purpose is to permit the discharge or escape of any air or steam in the system.

This pipe is often wrongfully described as the expansion pipe on the assumption that the expansion of the water in the system when it is heated will be taken up by this pipe and if necessary, expelled into the cold feed cistern. In point of fact this is not true because the expansion takes place in the cold feed pipe. Reference to Fig. 8A will show that in order for water to be discharged from the vent pipe it would have to be lifted the distance AB above the level of the water in the cold feed cistern. The fact that the vent pipe will be hot and the cold feed pipe cold, will only account for a difference of about 12 mm/300 mm of vertical distance be-

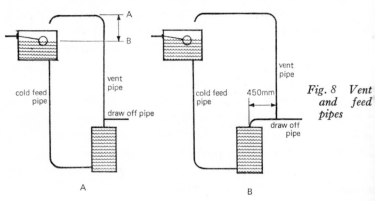

Fig. 8   Vent and feed pipes

tween cold water cistern and hot storage vessel. It is important that the vertical distance between the free surface of the cold water in the cistern and the turn-over of the vent pipe be greater than 12 mm/300 mm of vertical distance between cistern and storage vessel as otherwise discharge of hot water via the vent pipe into the cold water cistern will be liable to take place. The end of the vent pipe must not dip into the cold water in the cistern as otherwise siphonic action might feed cold water via the vent pipe to the top of the storage vessel.

The arrangement of vent pipe shown in Fig. 8A should preferably not be adopted as there will be single-pipe circulation leading to waste of electricity, a waste that can be avoided by introducing a length of horizontal pipe about 450 mm long before the vent pipe rises, as shown in Fig. 8B.

DRAW-OFF PIPING

In arranging the draw-off piping, two considerations should be borne in mind: first to have as short a 'dead leg' pipe to the kitchen sink as possible and secondly, to prevent single-pipe circulation. Much will depend upon the relative positions of the bath, sink and storage vessel. The storage vessel should be placed as near as possible to the sink, but care must be taken to avoid throwing away this advantage.

Usually, the size of draw-off pipe to the bath will be 22 mm while a 15 mm branch will be large enough for the sink where the pressure is greater. It is a mistake to feed the sink via the bath as

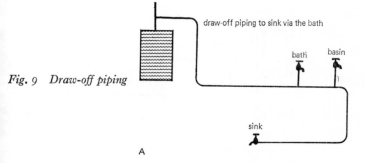

Fig. 9   Draw-off piping

shown in Fig. 9A. This arrangement is quite a usual one, but it is not satisfactory. In the first place, the draw-off pipe to the sink is needlessly long and a fair run of it is 28 mm in diameter, all of which goes to build up the 'dead leg' losses, and in the second place, the vent pipe rising vertically directly from the top of the storage vessel gives rise to single-pipe circulation. The best arrangement is shown in Fig. 9B where the draw-off pipe is taken from the storage vessel at low level and is extended by an internal

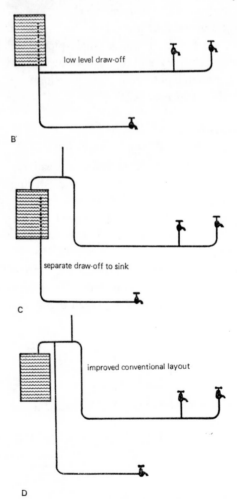

low level draw-off

B

separate draw-off to sink

C

improved conventional layout

D

stand pipe; the branch to the bathroom being taken off close to the storage vessel. This reduces the sink dead leg and prevents single-pipe circulation. An alternative is shown in Fig. 9c where a separate pipe to the sink is taken from the vessel at low level. Note how the vent pipe is arranged so as to prevent single-pipe circulation. If neither of these arrangements is possible and a more conventional arrangement is desired, the sink connection should be branched off the main draw-off pipe as soon as possible and should run by the shortest path to the sink tap as in Fig. 9d.

It used to be fairly common practice in solid-fuel installations for the draw-off to the kitchen to be taken off the flow pipe between boiler and storage vessel. With such an arrangement the sink tap will be fed partly with hot water from the top of the storage vessel flowing down the flow pipe and partly with water from the boiler flowing up the flow pipe. When the boiler is not in use, this latter supply will be cold, with the result that the sink tap will deliver a tepid mixture of hot and cold water. Such connections must be avoided wherever electric heating is adopted.

All that now remains to complete the installation is to fit the electric heater. This may be a horizontal immersion heater, a vertical circulator or even twin elements like the 'two-in-one' heater. It should not be forgotten that the effective hot storage capacity is that above the level of a horizontal heater or above the level of the bottom of a circulator, and that no part of a heater should be below the level of the cold feed.

In the case of a horizontal immersion heater, sufficient space between heater and bottom of the vessel must be allowed for the accumulation of scale and sludge.

If all the foregoing points are attended to, a simple straightforward solid fuel/electric system will result and, providing the hot storage vessel is properly insulated with three inches of approved insulating material, the standing losses will be not more than between one and one and a half units a day.

Such a system can be left switched on continuously under thermostatic control, and the full benefit of constant hot water on tap be experienced, without excessive running costs.

5 | Electric Water Heaters

In general there are two types of electric water heater, (1) the self-contained type consisting of storage cylinder, heating element, thermostat and pipe connections, together with thermal insulation and outer case, and (2) the immersion heater or circulator consisting of a heating element and thermostat for fixing into an existing hot storage vessel.

It should be understood that the heating element is common to both types, so that the following information on heating elements applies generally. In the self-contained electric water heater the position of the heating element and thermostat are fixed by the manufacturer, but the immersion heater or circulator can be fixed in any desired position.

ELECTRIC HEATING ELEMENTS

The heating or resistance wire in electric heating elements is almost invariably of nickel-chromium. There are two main types of elements distinguished by the fact that while one type can be withdrawn without the necessity for emptying the storage vessel, the other type cannot be removed without breaking a water joint.

The withdrawable type usually consists of a spiral of resistance wire mounted on a ceramic insulating former, the whole being inserted in a copper sheathing tube. In the other type the resistance wire is solidly embedded in a compressed insulating material within a flat blade or tubular sheath. The tubular sheathed variety usually employs a sheathing tube of about 12 mm diameter and can be bent or formed to almost any shape.

LOADING

The water heating elements that will be encountered in the water heating problems of the small house usually have loadings ranging from 500 to 3,000 watts according to requirements.

HEATING SURFACE

If it were possible to keep the heating surface of the water heating element free from scale, a very high loading of heating surface would be possible. In certain hard water districts, however, where the heater may become covered with scale, a loading density that would otherwise be quite satisfactory will result in the surface temperature of the element sheathing becoming dangerously high, so high in fact that it may exceed the melting point of the tin with which the sheaths are usually coated. The scale does not decrease the efficiency of the heater; with electricity the output of heat must be proportional to the input of electricity; but it does obstruct the transfer of heat from element to water and thus leads to a building-up of the temperature of both element-sheath and resistance wire. Excessive sheath temperatures result in conditions favourable to corrosion of the sheath whilst excessive resistance wire temperatures lead to danger of wire failing by burning out.

The watts density may be as high as 50 watts/645 mm^2 in the case of the tubular sheathed variety, but usually lies between 10 and 30 watts/645 mm^2 in the case of the withdrawable type.

SELF-DESCALING ELEMENTS

The usual shape of sheathed tube type of element shown in Fig. 10 is such that its expansion and contraction during heating and cooling is sufficient to fracture and throw off some, if not all, of the deposit of scale. Ample space round and below the element should be allowed for the accumulation of scale which may, with certain kinds of water, fall off in large flakes.

ACTION OF WATER ON THE SHEATHING METAL

Sheaths are usually made of copper and, as certain kinds of water are capable of dissolving copper, are usually tinned in order to prevent such action.

In hard water areas, the scale, as it is shed from the element by expansion and contraction, often takes off the tin with it and in time, the element may be completely de-tinned. Such action is hastened by overheating and softening of the tin coating.

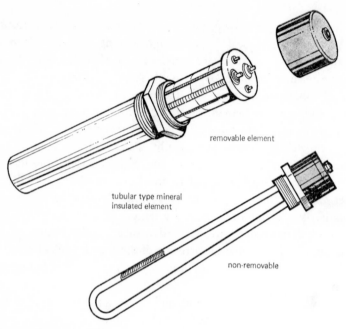

removable element

tubular type mineral
insulated element

non-removable

Fig. 10   Immersion heater

The life of a heating element depends very largely upon the type of scale that is formed, and it is consequently advisable to take advantage of the local experience of the Electricity Board in deciding the type of heater to use in any particular area.

THERMOSTATS

The type of thermostat used in water heating is of quite simple design. It consists of a tube and rod of metals having different thermal coefficients of expansion and the relative movement of these two pieces of metal is made to operate the switch portion of the instrument.

Thermostats should comply with the appropriate BS DESIGN: Section 2B, and must be of suitable capacity to deal with the loading of the heating element.

Where the supply of electricity is A.C., by far the greater majority of thermostats have micro-gap contacts with some kind of device which gives the contacts a quick 'make and break' action.

In breaking the circuit the contacts are moved only a very short distance apart, hence the term 'micro-gap'. This distance in itself is not sufficient to extinguish the arc that is set up as the circuit is broken. The extinguishing of the arc is done automatically by the alternations of the supply when the pressure during the cycle reaches zero; this happens 100 times a second. The contacts themselves are relatively large in size and thus cool the arc to such an extent that it is prevented from re-striking when the voltage reaches its maximum figure again.

The micro-gap thermostat is sometimes used on a D.C. supply with a condenser of one or two microfarads capacity connected across the contacts, but this practice is not recommended by the makers.

Another type of thermostat which is sometimes employed makes use of a mercury tube which is tilted by the action of the bimetallic rod; the mercury in the tube making and breaking contact.

Mercury tube thermostats are suitable for either A.C. or D.C. but are not so compact in size as the micro-gap type and must, of course, be installed the proper way up and be in correct alignment.

THERMOSTAT DIFFERENTIAL

The word 'differential' is used to describe the number of degrees between the temperature at which a thermostat switches the supply off and the temperature at which it switches it on again. Other things being equal the differential depends upon the length of the thermostat stem. Common values are from 5 to 10°C for lengths up to 300 mm and 3 to 5°C for longer stems. The effect of a deposit of scale on a thermostat is to widen the differential.

There is no particular object in having a very small differential in water heating as there is no need for the temperature to be controlled very precisely. It will, of course, be appreciated that the smaller the differential, the more frequently the heating element will be switched on and off. On the other hand, if the differential is too large the temperature of the water when drawn off just before the thermostat is due to cut in will be unduly low and the output of hot water will thus be reduced.

A thermostat is affected by the average temperature of the whole of its operating length and thermostats that are fitted horizontally in hot water vessels function rather differently from those that are fitted vertically.

If a long thermostat which extends practically the whole length of a storage vessel is fitted vertically, the temperature at which it operates will be in effect the average temperature of the water in the vessel. A short thermostat fitted vertically will only be affected by the water in the lower or upper half of the vessel, depending upon whether the thermostat is fitted from the top or the bottom. Consequently, with vertical fixing, the longest thermostat that can be accommodated is the best in every case.

If small quantities of hot water are drawn off at frequent intervals from a storage vessel fitted with a vertical thermostat, it is quite possible for the water at the top of the vessel to be boiling although the mean temperature, which is the temperature that affects the thermostat, is lower than the temperature for which it is set.

When the thermostat is fixed horizontally, it will obviously be affected only by the temperature of the layer of water with which it is surrounded. If used as it normally will be with a horizontally fixed heating element, it will operate as soon as the temperature of the body of water above its own level reaches the cut-out temperature because the horizontal arrangement of the heater tends to raise gradually the temperature of the whole body of water above its level. It will thus be seen that the temperature marked on the dial of a thermostat will be approximately correct if the thermostat is fixed horizontally in conjunction with a horizontal heating element, but if it is fixed vertically the temperature of the water at the top of the vessel will probably be in excess of that shown on the dial.

The setting of a thermostat should always be checked before any installation is handed over owing to the possibility of the instrument having been damaged during transit. In hard water districts the thermostat setting should not exceed 60°C. Higher settings are permissible in soft water districts, but the setting should not be higher than is necessary to ensure a satisfactory supply of hot water, in order to avoid unnecessary heat losses.

POSITION OF THE HEATING ELEMENTS

Heating elements may be fitted in three different positions in the hot water storage vessel, i.e.:

(a) Horizontally through the side
(b) vertically through the top
(c) vertically through the bottom

In each case the heating element is fitted internally into the storage vessel and the amount of heat actually transferred to the water will be the same however it is fitted. There will, however, be a considerable variation in the way in which the water is heated and in the temperature of the water at various levels in the vessel.

Horizontal Entry

If the heating element is fixed horizontally from the side (see Fig. 11A) there will be a tolerably rapid and general circulation of the water within the vessel with the result that in a given time a large volume of water is heated through a small number of degrees. This means that there will be a relatively small difference in temperature between the top and bottom of the vessel and there will be a tendency for the whole content of the vessel to be gradually heated. Water that is below the level of the heating element will remain practically unheated and consequently the heater should be fixed low down in the vessel.

With this arrangement of heating element, it is usual for the thermostat to be fixed horizontally and slightly above the level of the heating element. When in this position it will switch off the heating element as soon as the layer of water in which it is fixed reaches the temperature for which it is set.

When the heating element is cut out, the temperature of the water at the top of the vessel will be slightly higher than the cut-out temperature and the layer of water between the level of the

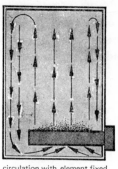

circulation with element fixed
horizontally

A

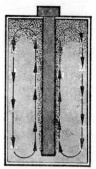

circulation with element
fixed vertically from
the top

B

Fig. 11   Position of elements

heating element and that of the thermostat will be at a slightly
lower temperature.

The water below the heating element will be practically unheated and it would be clearly useless to fix the thermostat below
the level of the heater.

The mounting of the heating element and thermostat in one
head simplifies fixing because only one hole in the storage vessel
has to be provided and in practice this arrangement is satisfactory.

Vertical Top Entry
If the heating element is fixed vertically from the top as in Fig. 11B
it must be long enough to extend sufficiently far downwards to
heat the required volume of water, as water below the level of
the heater will not be heated. In this case, the water heated by the
element rises vertically and as it will be in contact with the heater
all the way to the top, it is obvious that each portion of the element
will heat still further the ascending column of hot water. The
result is that a relatively small quantity of water is in circulation
and that this small quantity of water will absorb the whole output
of the heating element with the result that hot water will collect
in a layer at the top of the storage vessel, there being a considerable

temperature difference between the water at the top and bottom of the vessel.

As time goes on the depth of the layer of hot water increases until the whole of the water above the level of the bottom of the heater is heated. It is thus seen that by this method of fixing, a small quantity of hot water is obtained in a relatively short space of time.

When the heating element is fixed vertically from the top it is usual for the thermostat to be fixed in the same position and the length of the thermostat should be proportional to the length of the heating element. If the length of the thermostat is much shorter than the heating element, the heating element will be switched off before the water below the level of the thermostat is fully heated.

The thermostat will cut-out when the average temperature of the water surrounding it reaches the cut-out temperature and a high temperature at the top end of the thermostat will be counteracted by a low temperature at the bottom.

Vertical Bottom Entry

If the heater is fitted vertically from the bottom of the vessel, the way in which the water is heated will be a compromise between horizontal fixing and vertical fixing from the top. If the heating element is long and extends nearly to the top of the vessel there will be little difference between this arrangement and vertical top entry. On the other hand, if the heating element is short and does not extend far above the bottom of the vessel, the heating effect will not be very different from that of the horizontal arrangement except that there will be rather more tendency for a layer of hot water to be formed at the top of the vessel.

As in other cases the thermostat will normally be placed in the same position as the heating element and should be as long as possible. If the thermostat is very short, drawing off a relatively small quantity of water will cause the thermostat to cut in and it is possible that the amount of heat added to the water before the thermostat cuts out again will exceed the amount of heat in the water drawn off. If this is so, continual drawing of small quantities of hot water will gradually build up the temperature at the top of the vessel and may lead to boiling.

SELF-CONTAINED WATER HEATERS

The term 'self-contained' is used to distinguish the complete factory-made assembly of vessel, heater and thermostat together with its insulation and outer case from the installation where an immersion heater or circulator is fixed on site into an ordinary hot storage vessel that is usually part of an existing solid-fuel hot water supply system.

Self-contained electric water heaters should comply with BS 3456, Section A13, and BS 843 which lays down details of size, performance, and screwed connections for piping.

It is advisable to consult the attractive technical literature issued by manufacturers of water heaters before deciding on the type to use for any specific purpose.

Self-contained electric water heaters can be classified broadly as:
(a) 'Non-pressure' or 'open outlet'-type which are controlled from the inlet side and supply one point only.
(b) 'Pressure'-type heaters which will work under pressure from a feed cistern and are intended to supply one or more taps.
(c) Cistern-type water heaters incorporating a self-contained cold water cistern arranged for direct connection to the cold water main and serving one or more taps.
(d) Two-in-one water heaters provided with two heating elements and serving one or more taps. This type is designed primarily for installation in close proximity to the kitchen sink.

NON-PRESSURE TYPE HEATERS

Non-pressure type heaters are fitted with open outlets and have the controlling tap on the inlet side so that they may be connected directly to the cold water mains.

The top of the container is usually vented with the double object of preventing pressure building up should the outlet become obstructed, possibly by scale, and of preventing the formation of a vacuum through the action of the draw-off pipe. Fig. 12

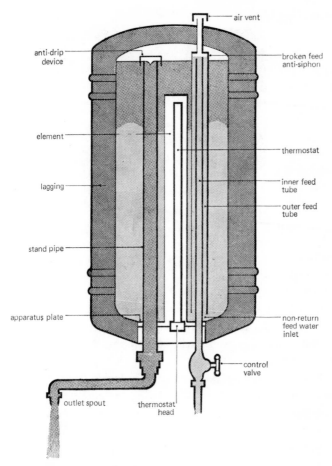

air vent

anti-drip device

broken feed anti-siphon

element

thermostat

lagging

inner feed tube

outer feed tube

stand pipe

apparatus plate

non-return feed water inlet

control valve

outlet spout

thermostat head

Fig. 12   Open outlet sink heater

shows a typical 'open outlet' sink heater incorporating an anti-siphonic cold water inlet pipe which prevents the content of the vessel being drawn back into the cold water main.

As water expands approximately 4 per cent in volume when heated through a temperature rise of 80°C dripping will take place from the open outlet of a non-pressure type heater unless some means are employed to prevent it.

Various forms of anti-drip devices are employed, one being a

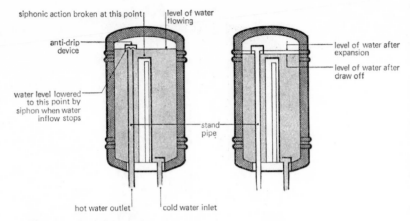

Fig. 13   Anti-drip device

siphonic trap formed at the top of the outlet pipe as in Fig. 13 so that when the tap is turned off, the level of the water in the container drops slightly to allow for subsequent expansion without dripping from the outlet. This, of course, means that when the tap is turned on there will be a slight delay before water flows from the heater and that water will continue to flow for a short time after the tap is closed.

The satisfactory working of such a device depends to a great extent upon the flow of water being maintained at a constant figure and consequently it is usual for a restricting device to be fitted to the inlet tap.

Some water authorities insist on a siphonic anti-drip device being provided, but others who recognize the fact that with the siphonic anti-drip device the user cannot draw very small quantities of water from the heater and that the siphon is apt to become choked with scale in hard water districts, permit single-point heaters to be connected provided that they have an air seal fitted to the end of the spout as in Fig. 14. This type of heater has a clear waterway at the top of the standpipe and, in action, is completely filled with water up to the spout. The construction of the air seal keeps air from ascending the stand pipe and thus prevents displacement of the water.

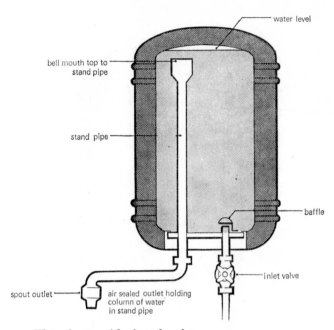

Fig. 14   Water heater with air seal outlet

Another design is made with the ejector device shown in Fig. 15 which consists of an anti-drip chamber inside the heater adjacent to the cold water inlet. When at rest this chamber is filled with water approximately equal in content to the expansion of the whole of the water in the cistern. When the inlet valve is open, the incoming water exerts a suction upon the contents of the chamber and empties it. When the inlet valve is closed, the water in the heater finds its way back by gravity into the chamber which, when filled, reduces the level of the water in the heater well below the stand pipe. It is impossible, therefore, for the water heater to drip, provided the waterways to and from the anti-drip chamber remain clear. As the water in this part of the heater is comparatively low in temperature, there is little danger of scaling even when hard water is used.

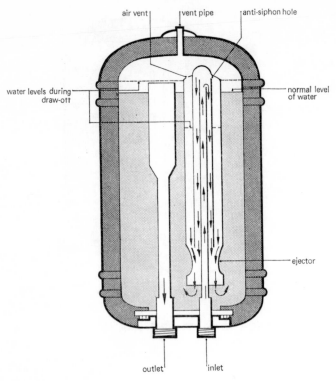

Fig. 15   Water heater with ejector anti-drip

PRESSURE-TYPE HEATERS
Pressure-type heaters are designed to work under the head from a cold water feed cistern at high level provided this does not exceed 18 m and to supply any normal number of taps.

Figure 16 shows a typical pressure-type heater. The smallest multipoint heater in general use is the 55 litres size in view of the fact that this is the smallest size capable of giving one bath.

Pressure-type water heaters are controlled from the outlet side and, consequently, no anti-drip device is required.

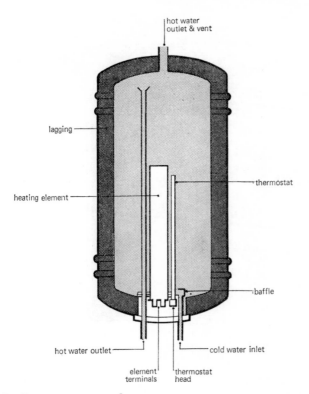

Fig. 16   Pressure-type water heater

CISTERN-TYPE WATER HEATERS

These heaters are also suitable for supplying any normal number of taps. They consist essentially of a pressure-type heater fitted with a ball-valve feed cistern at the top of its casing. A cistern-type heater therefore forms a complete hot water system in itself, needing no external vent pipe and being suitable, subject to the water authority's requirements, for direct connection to the main. It must, however, be fixed above the level of the highest tap which it has to supply. Owing to the internal pressure being limited to the small head of water provided by the feed cistern, the storage vessel can be made in rectangular shape, thus reducing the projection from the wall, a useful feature where space is limited.

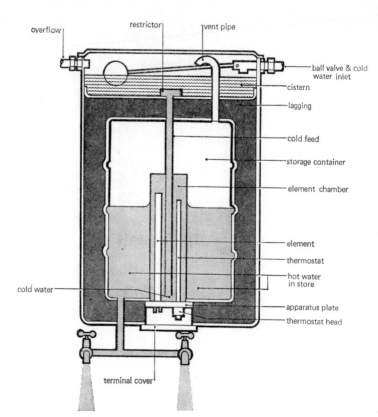

Fig. 17   Cistern-type water heater

There are two types of cistern heater:

(a) Constant volume and varying temperature type.

(b) Constant temperature and varying volume type.

The first, shown in Fig. 17, operates in precisely the same way as a pressure type heater.

The second type works on the principle of restricting the flow of cold water into the heater to an amount that can be heated immediately to whatever storage temperature is desired or, in other words, by heating the water to the required temperature as it is admitted. The stored hot water is obtained not by displace-

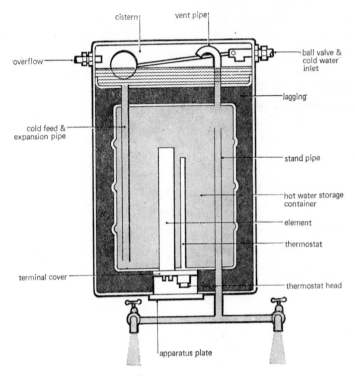

Fig. 18   Cistern-type water heater

ment by cold water but by emptying the storage vessel so that the water level in the vessel falls as water is drawn off. With this type of heater the draw-off pipe is taken from the bottom of the storage vessel. Such heaters must be designed so that the heating element is always surrounded with water and an arrangement whereby this can be done without reducing the useful storage capacity of the vessel is shown in Fig. 18. The heating element is housed in an inner chamber arranged in such a way that the chamber remains full of water whatever the level of the water in the storage vessel itself. This type of heater never runs cold so long as it is switched on, but when the stored hot water has been drawn off the flow will be reduced to almost a trickle.

THE TWO-IN-ONE HEATER

This heater is of the pressure type and is manufactured in two
different sizes, 90 and 136 litre. The special feature about this
type of heater is that it has twin thermostatically controlled
elements one of which, usually of 2,500 watts loading, is placed
in the conventional position at low level in the storage vessel
whilst the other is fitted at such a level that it heats approximately
five or six gallons of water. Fig. 19 shows a typical two-in-one
heater.

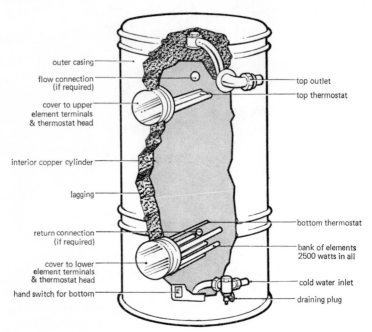

Fig. 19   Two-in-one water heater

In normal operation the upper heating element is kept switched
on permanently under thermostatic control whilst the lower
element is only switched on when a larger quantity of water is
required for baths or washing day.

This arrangement reduces the consumption of electricity in
two ways. First, the heat losses from the storage vessel are reduced

because of the smaller quantity of water that is kept at the storage temperature and, secondly, economy in the use of hot water is more or less enforced.

With the two-in-one heater constant hot water on tap throughout the house is provided, but the amount of hot water that is normally available at any time is limited to approximately 28 litres. This is ample for general purposes, but it will be appreciated that where the quantity is not restricted there will always be a tendency for more to be used.

INLET BAFFLES

All types of water heaters have some kind of device such as illustrated in Fig. 20 to prevent the incoming cold water from cooling the storage unduly. The baffle usually employed is fitted at the cold water entry so as to deflect the incoming water to the bottom of the storage vessel.

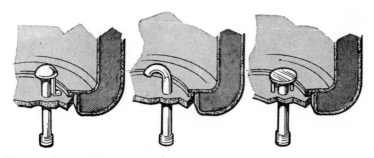

Fig. 20   Inlet baffles for water heaters

PACKAGED PLUMBING UNIT

A self-contained unit for providing both hot and cold water for bath, basin, kitchen sink and w.c. It comprises a cold water cistern, hot water container and pipework built into and within a rigid framework (see Fig. 21).

This unit is based on a design developed by the Research and Development Group of the Ministry of Housing and Local Government, and is acceptable for the appropriate Government grants.

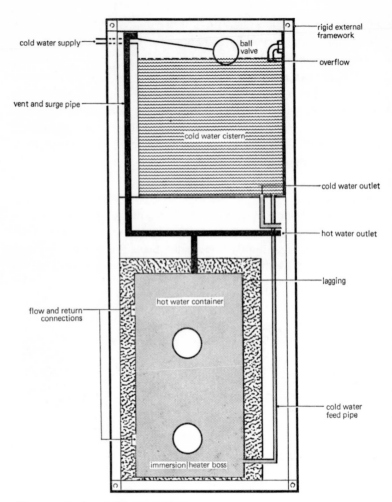

Fig. 21   Packaged Plumbing Unit

It is readily handled up stairs and through doorways. It may be installed in a cupboard, against a wall, in a passage or convenient corner, or incorporated in the structure of new buildings.

The plumbing unit only needs connecting to main water supply, electricity supply and services as shown in the accompanying diagrams, see Fig. 22A and B. There are alternative capacities

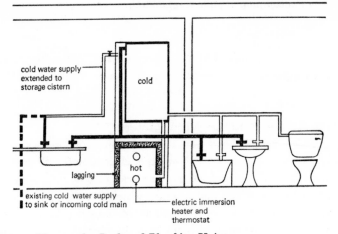

cold water supply
extended to
storage cistern

cold

lagging

hot

existing cold water supply
to sink or incoming cold main

electric immersion
heater and
thermostat

Fig. 22   The use of a Packaged Plumbing Unit
   A Installation with all services on one floor
   B Installation serving 2 floors and showing alternative connection
      with back boiler

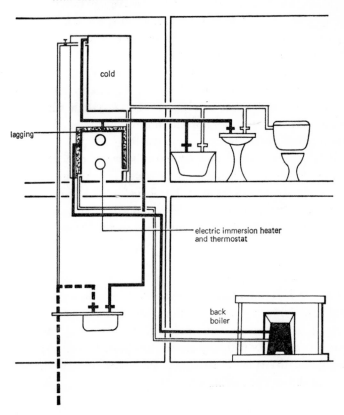

cold

lagging

electric immersion heater
and thermostat

back
boiler

available with a basic design of a 230 litres cold water storage cistern supplying a 115 or 230 litre hot water storage cylinder.

Water Heating and the White Meter

The White Meter tariff—so called because of the distinctive colour of the meters installed—meters electricity for all purposes at two different cost rates, a day rate and a night rate. Any electricity used during the night period which is commonly between 11 p.m. and 9 a.m. will be charged at the low rate. At other times electricity will cost slightly more than the normal domestic tariff.

To get maximum benefit from the White Meter tariff, the customer must be able to heat a substantial proportion of his water on the cheap night-time rate. An average family uses about 136 to 159 litres of hot water a day. Ideally, the hot water storage capacity of a water heater for White Meter should be as large as possible according to the space available.

Each night the time switch controlling water heating will switch on to heat at the cheap rate. This leads to a basic design criterion for White Meter water heating. Design a system with sufficient storage capacity to cater for the normal needs of the maximum size of family likely to live in the dwelling.

It is not unusual for new homes to be provided with a 226 litre storage cylinder. If this supply of water is exhausted during the day some water will have to be heated at the higher, day-time rate. There are a number of self-contained water heaters available which are specially designed for use with the White Meter tariff.

MULTIPLE INSTALLATIONS

Although it is important to provide sufficient water heated on the night-time rate to cater for the main demand of the following day, it is not essential to provide all this water for the main storage vessel. As with any electrically heated water system, additional 'on the spot' heaters may be placed to avoid long 'dead legs' or difficult plumbing situations.

TWO HEATER CYLINDER

Undoubtedly, the most economical way to provide adequate hot water for a family on the White Meter tariff, is to fit a cylinder of around 226 litres capacity. However, there may not be sufficient space to install a cylinder of this size, and it may be necessary to limit the cylinder to a maximum of 159 litres. If the household will not generally require more than 159 litres of hot water a day, this will be quite satisfactory. If it is only necessary to heat the tank on day-time electricity to supplement the night-time charge, say once a week for the extra demand on laundry day, the average cost of electricity per unit will be near the night-time price per unit.

With only one immersion heater at the base of the storage vessel, the whole water content would be heated each time the electricity was switched on. This system would become uneconomic if the supply of hot water heated during the nights ran out frequently, and day-time boosts became a regular requirement.

To ensure that only a limited amount of water is heated on the day-time rate, a second immersion heater may be fitted to the tank in a position where it will heat about 56 litres of water, before its own thermostat switches off the supply of electricity. The second immersion heater may also be manually controlled, but it will generally be more sensible for the user to leave it on all the time, since its built-in thermostat will keep it switched off until it is needed. As long as there is more than 56 litres of hot water left in the tank from the previous off-peak night-rate charge this second heater will not switch on.

It is recommended that there shall be a minimum difference of 10°C between the settings of the thermostats of the upper and lower immersion heaters. In soft water areas the thermostat on the lower immersion heater should be set at 70°C and the thermostat on the upper immersion heater at 60°C. In hard water areas these settings should be reduced by up to 10°C.

The minimum amount of hot water required for a bath is selected as being 56 litres—the usual last requirement of the day. The following table indicates the approximate proportions of night-time electricity, and day-time electricity used with a two heater cylinder. The high level element will be located to provide 56 litres of hot water in each instance. These figures are intended as a guide only, and are the result of practical trials, with the

Size of tank (litres)	Low level element % night units	High level element % day units
113	60	40
136	70	30
159	80	20
226	95	5

high level heater under thermostatic control only. It will be seen from the table that even a 226 litre cylinder may sometimes need 'topping up' on day-time electricity. Since the larger cylinder could occasionally heat all of its 226 litres on day-time electricity if it were not fitted with a second heater, it could be said to be the instance where it is most important to install a second immersion heater, if there is any possibility of 226 litres being insufficient.

General Rule: Install a second immersion heater whenever possible in any cylinder if there is any possibility of the total capacity being exhausted early in the day.

IMMERSION HEATERS FOR A TWO HEATER CYLINDER

The upper immersion heater in a two heater cylinder will need to keep up with demand, as far as possible, and should therefore be rated at 3 kilowatts. This will provide the fastest possible response.

The lower heater, however, has a period of approximately 8 hours in which to heat a tank full of water. In most installations, no water will be drawn off during this time, and it will only be necessary to fit a heater sufficiently large to heat the whole contents of the cylinder in, say 6 or 7 hours. Some margin of error must be allowed for standing losses during this time.

Size of tank (litres)	Rating of low level element for White Meter
113	1·5 kW
136	1·5 kW
159	1·5 kW
226	3·0 kW

GOOD INSTALLATION

Because water heated at night on the White Meter tariff must still be hot enough for a bath in the evening, a water heating installation for this tariff must be well designed. All losses must be minimized, particularly those from mixing and single pipe circulation. The storage cylinder must be very well insulated.

6 | Water Heating by Gas

The main advantages of using gas for water heating are

1 It is clean, creates no dust or mess in the house and it conforms with the Clean Air Act. As it comes straight from a pipe it needs no storage space.

2 The hot flame of gas properly regulated heats water very fast. The instantaneous heaters provide hot water in an endless supply. The water in storage systems quickly reheats as the supply is drawn from the tank.

3 Automatic controls permit close regulation of the fuel used and allow adjustments to meet the needs of a family.

4 High efficiency of appliances reduces running costs.

5 A gas water heater may be fixed at the very point the hot water is required enabling a certain flexibility in house design and a reduction in the cost of plumbing work.

Selection of a Heater

The output of a water heater is relative to the given rate of water flow and temperature rise, and although the supply of water at any required temperature is continuous, the speed of delivery is limited by the capacity of the heater. For example, although a large heater will give hot water more quickly than a smaller one the latter will give greater efficiency and at less cost for small intermittent demands. The main consideration in selecting a heater is that it will provide the required amount of hot water to meet the demands of the family at peak times.

INSTANTANEOUS HEATERS

These heaters will give a continuous flow of hot water at any time within a few seconds of turning on any tap to which the heater is connected. The temperature of the water is variable according to the temperature of the cold feed, most heaters being designed to give a 26°C temperature rise. Models are available which control the water flow to give a constant outlet temperature. The flow is limited at the maximum temperature available at any time but it is usually possible to obtain a greater flow at a lower temperature without any drop in the efficiency of the heater.

Apart from the small consumption of the pilot jet, gas is used only when the water is flowing from a tap. It is the most economical form of heater and the single point type has the lowest running cost of any gas water heater. Capital and installation costs are generally less than for storage heaters giving equivalent service but the high gas rate might possibly require the fitting of larger services pipes and meters.

Since the satisfactory operation of an instantaneous heater depends on a minimum flow of water it is essential that the pressure head of the water supply is adequate. This will vary with each type of appliance and the help of the local gas regional office should be sought.

Thermostatic controls are fitted to some models ensuring that the water is supplied at a constant temperature. The correct adjustment of instantaneous heaters is more critical than that of other types and this means regular servicing is necessary to their functioning.

Some models have balanced flues which eliminate the need for a conventional chimney. Balanced flue heaters are room sealed and must be fitted to an outside wall. The air enters and the exhaust gases pass out through the balanced flue which is completely sealed off from the room itself. The heater is therefore unaffected by room ventilation and exhaust gases cannot enter the room.

It is important to know that only balanced flue heaters must be used for new installations in bathrooms.

Single-point heaters over a sink or washbasin must always be fitted within an arm's length (about 0·6 m) of the draw-off point. Where this is not possible the multi-point type must be used even if it is supplying only one draw-off, the reason being the danger of a spout longer than that could suffer mechanical damage because it would be unsupported along its length. Multi-point heaters are connected to the fittings they serve by means of pipes which discharge through taps as for any other piped supply. The pipes of course can be supported by clips or brackets.

Instantaneous water heaters for the bathroom can be provided with an extended swivel spout to serve the bath and the wash-basin provided it does not exceed 0·6 m in length. The heater must of course be fitted with a balanced flue.

STORAGE HEATERS

These units comprise a heater combined with an insulated storage vessel that will retain heated water over a period of time against a future demand. The volume of hot water they can supply is limited by the capacity, so the size of the unit must be selected carefully to meet peak demands. If it is properly sized it is un-likely that its full capacity will be used at any one time but should this occur, then the good stratification obtained with a gas storage water heater ensures that small quantities of hot water are available again within a short time. This also applies when the heater is first lit. They can be either floor standing or wall mounted and must generally be connected to a cistern supply. Some types are available with an integral feed cistern and provided these are fitted above the level of the highest draw-off tap, it will not be necessary to fit an additional feed cistern.

Sink storage heaters are available for fixing to the wall above the sink and discharge by a swivel spout of not greater than 0·6 m in length.

GAS CIRCULATORS

These are in effect, miniature gas boilers usually fitted near the hot water storage cylinder. A circulator is an economical way of converting an existing water system to gas or of providing an entirely new system. Thermostatically controlled they can also be provided with an economy valve which can be set to either heat the whole tank, or keep a few litres of water at the top of the storage cylinder constantly hot.

GAS BOILERS

Several types of gas boilers are available and they are ideal for a busy household needing a great deal of hot water and especially so when the prime purpose is space heating.

The modern gas boiler is a sophisticated appliance being fully automatic in action and capable of being set to follow a specific programme to the clock, making it economical to run.

The boiler indirectly heats the water in the storage cylinder whilst circulating hot water to the radiators around the house.

A modern innovation is the gas back-boiler which is an ideal replacement for the solid fuel back-boiler. It is possible to install a very modern gas-fire and boiler with the minimum alterations to the existing pipework. The boiler is capable of providing reasonable central heating as well as hot water for domestic usage. The fire and the boiler are separately controlled and they may be used together or independently.

New design principles have enabled gas boilers to be housed in a very limited space without reducing their capacity to provide hot water. They can be wall mounted in the kitchen or anywhere else. They must of course be fixed to an outside wall.

Installation of Gas Appliances

The installation of gas piping and appliances must be carried out by skilled men who have a complete knowledge of the technical and safety requirements involved. They must have the proper tools and testing equipment, and the householder should know that under the Gas Safety Regulations 1972 it is in fact specified that only competent persons shall carry out gas installation work.

CORGI

The Gas Corporation in conjunction with a number of Trade Associations have set up a voluntary organization to maintain proper standards in all gas work. It is known as the Confederation for the Registration of Gas Installers and has assumed the abbreviated title of CORGI. Every plumber who contracts to do gas installation work should be registered under the scheme and householders should insist that any gas work carried out in their homes is undertaken by CORGI members only. Lists of members can be inspected at the Gas Showrooms. Every Registered CORGI gas installing business undertakes to perform gas installation and service work complying with British Standard Codes of Practice, Building Regulations and Gas Corporation requirements.

THE GAS ACT

Plumbers and householders should know that the Gas Act became Law on 1 January 1973 and Regulations under this Act give powers to designated officers of the Gas Corporation to enter premises and cut off a supply if in the opinion of these accredited officers an installation is unsafe.

RELEVANT CODES OF PRACTICE

The following BSI Codes of Practice should be referred to when installing gas supply and appliances.

CP 331 Pt. 1 1957   Installation of pipes and meters for town gas. Part 1: Service Pipes.

CP 331 Pt. 2 1965   Installation of pipes and meters for town gas. Part 2: Metering and meter control.

CP 331 Pt. 3 1965   Installation of pipes and meters for town gas. Part 3: Installation pipes.

CP 332 Pt. 1 1961   Selection and installation of town gas space heating. Part 1: Independent domestic appliances.

CP 332 Pt. 2 1964   Selection and installation of town gas space heating. Part 2: Central heating boilers for domestic premises.

CP 333 Pt. 1 1964   Selection and installation of town gas hot water supplies. Part 1: Domestic premises.

SEVEN POINTS FOR WATER HEATER INSTALLATION

1.   The site should be well-ventilated and convenient for connection to an existing flue where this is applicable. It should be noted, however, that if the appliance is to replace an existing water heater in a bathroom, only room sealed models should be used.

2. It is preferable to keep the pipe run to the main point of usage as short as possible to minimize heat losses.

3. The existing gas installation pipes should be checked for soundness and adequacy of supply, and where applicable the flue should be checked for sufficient 'pull', correct size and suitable termination.

4. The head of water should be sufficient to operate the appliance as laid down in the manufacturer's instructions.

5. The appliance should be fixed securely and after connection to the gas and water supplies, the installation should be tested for soundness. The gas and water rates should then be adjusted to conform with the maker's instructions.

6. Check that the appliance controls are operating correctly.

7. Finally, instruct the customer on the use of the appliance referring to the manufacturer's instructions.

EIGHT POINTS FOR SPACE HEATER INSTALLATION

1. Before installation, check the chimney (flueway) for 'pull'. This can be done by holding a match near it. The flue is operating satisfactorily if the flame is drawn into the flueway. If it burns steadily, check for restrictions in the flue; if the flame blows back, the flue is subject to down draught and may need modifications.

2. Make sure that the chimney has been swept if the fire is being sited into an open fireplace and remove or wedge fully open any damper, register plate or canopy in the fireplace opening. Make sure that there is adequate clearance at the rear and/or sides of the gas fire flue spigot (refer to the manufacturer's instructions).

3. Check that the existing installation pipes are sound and are of adequate size.

4. When fixing the appliance a filling in or closure plate must always be fitted. This is designed to improve the performance of the appliance. It consists usually of two openings, the top one being for the flue spigot and the lower one to provide a flue break and to assist in room ventilation. Plates are usually obtained from the appliance manufacturer or else the type is specified in the manufacturer's fixing instructions.

5.   Space heaters must stand on a non-combustible material which extends 152 mm either side of the space heater and 304 mm from the back of the fireplace and is at least 15 mm thick. If the space heater is being wall mounted there should be a distance of at least 228 mm from the burner manifold and the floor level.

6.   The space heater must be fitted level using the correct type of fittings and pipe as specified by the local Gas Board.

7.   Test the finished installation for soundness and check the gas rate using the meter test dial and a stopwatch, and ensure that this is in accordance with the manufacturer's instructions. The gas rate can be calculated using the following formula:

$$\text{Gas rate} = \frac{\text{Heat input}}{\text{Calorific value of the gas}}$$

Instruct the customer on the operation of the appliance.

FIVE POINTS FOR COOKER INSTALLATION

1.   The siting of the appliance must be carefully considered, bearing in mind the following points:

(a) it should be in a well-ventilated position;

(b) there should be sufficient natural light to ensure that it can be used with safety;

(c) there should be sufficient clearance to ensure that it can be used without obstruction, in other words there should be room to open the oven door;

(d) it should be in a convenient position for use by the customer, i.e. near to preparation space.

4.   Follow the maker's instructions carefully when assembling the appliance. Check that the existing installation pipes are sound and are of adequate size.

3.   When connecting the appliance use only recommended fittings, ensuring that there is a means of disconnection. The appliance must be fitted level—this is important for all appliances but particularly in the case of cookers where pans of liquid will be placed on them.

4. When the appliance has been connected again test the installation for soundness. Check that the appliance controls are functioning correctly and test any concealed supplies on the appliance for soundness, i.e. the grill and oven supplies.

5. Before leaving the premises ensure that pilots have been relit and above all explain the operation of the appliance in detail to the customer. Suggest that the customer operates the appliance after instruction to ensure that he or she has understood the explanation; and give the customer the manufacturer's customer instruction leaflet for future reference. It is advisable not to leave the fitting instructions with the customer as this may tempt do-it-yourself enthusiasts to attempt any servicing or repair work.

GAS SUPPLY

The gas meter should be capable of passing the full consumption of the heater in addition to the requirements of all other appliances, and it is preferable to run an independent supply from the meter to the heater. If this is not possible it will be advisable to ensure that the heater receives the first delivery of gas from the meter, and that the pipe sizes are adequate to give a full gas supply irrespective of demands.

A full-bore gas cock should be fitted close to appliances to facilitate maintenance without interrupting the gas supply to other parts of the house.

COLD WATER SUPPLY

To ensure a constant pressure and flow of water to a water heater it should be fed by a single pipe from the storage cistern of the house. In certain circumstances mains water supply may be used but it is always advisable to consult the local water undertaking on this point.

The most important considerations are to see to it that

(a) pipe sizes are adequate to pass the required water flow at the prevailing pressure

(b) pipe runs are as short as possible and,

(c) a fixed jumper stopcock of an approved pattern is fitted on the cold water inlet as close as possible to the heater to isolate it when repairs are necessary.

HOT WATER DRAW-OFF

The pipe run should be as short as possible to avoid heat loss and waste of water. The most used draw-off point should have the shortest run. In no case should the maximum pipe run exceed 8 m.

Single point heaters have open outlet spouts and on no account should any additional fittings or other obstruction be connected to the outlet side of the heater. Any such connection would result in damage to the heating body.

VENTILATION

The ventilation requirements for heater compartments and various types of rooms are under constant review by technical committees concerned with gas installation. As knowledge of this complex subject increases, amendments to the regulations are made. It is advisable for the installer to keep himself up-to-date with the regulations issued from the Gas Corporation Research and Development Department.

FLUES

The installer is very much concerned with flues and should have a sound knowledge of their basic principles because of the safety factors involved.

In any fuel burning appliance, the hot products of combustion being less dense than air, will have a tendency to flow upwards in a flue or chimney. With a modern high efficiency gas water heater, so much heat is removed from the product of combustion that it is of the utmost importance to plan the flue in such a way to fully conserve the residual heat of the product and to ensure that no resistance is offered to the free flow of flue gases. A permanent state of down-draught can be set up which the heater may be unable to overcome due to the excessive cooling of the flue gases— for example, in a long length of flue exposed outside a building.

The Flue Terminal

The flue terminal should offer the minimum resistance to combustion products and have a free area equal at least to twice the nominal area of the flue.

There should be outlets on opposite, or all sides except where the design is such as to provide extraction under all wind conditions.

It should have effective protection against entry of birds, leaves, rain or snow, and the minimum dimension of any opening should be not less than 6·35 mm or greater than 14·3 mm.

Construction of the Flue

The material of the flue must be resistant to temperatures up to 95°C. It must have low conductivity and be resistant to acids. This precludes the use of untreated metal flues.

The flue must be run as far as possible under cover to minimize cooling.

The flue must be of the specified size and there must be no reduction in the cross-sectional area at any point. The ideal shape is circular and this should be adhered to as far as practical.

The interior surface of the flue must be smooth and free from projections, and there should be a rising tendency along its entire length and sharp changes of direction avoided. The horizontal length of the flue should not exceed 1·20 m.

If the flue is of excessive length or if for any reason the flue gases are likely to become cooled below the dewpoint, provision must be made for disposal of the condensate.

Excessive dilution of the products of combustion with cool air should be avoided and this precludes the use of common flues, open tees or any form of extra air inlet.

In the case of persistent down-draught or where static conditions are encountered, the flue installation must be re-designed to conform to the foregoing principles.

Balanced Flues

The development of the balanced flue has enabled the fixing of water heaters in positions not suitable for the more conventional type of appliance. The balanced flue heater does not need a draught diverter nor any additional flue equipment inside the room. It therefore presents a neat appearance and is more easily fitted where headroom is limited.

Balanced flue terminals should not be fitted in any position which would allow combustion products to feed back through adjacent doors or windows. These positions include, immediately beneath eaves or a balcony, at a re-entrant position on the face of the building, or adjacent to any projection on the face of the building.

Other advantages are:

(a) They can be installed in positions not suitable for conventional water heaters.

(b) A balanced flue heater does not need a draught diverter nor any additional flue equipment inside the room; it, therefore, presents a neat appearance, and is more easily fitted where headroom is limited.

(c) The terminal is fairly inconspicuous, and vertical flue pipe is not required. This is particularly important in new housing and has been welcomed by architects.

Water Heaters as Auxiliaries

A multi-point heater may be connected to a boiler system as an alternative and continuous source of hot water supply during the summer months, and is similarly available for immediate use whenever the boiler is inoperative. The combined installation of heater and boiler is simple as the same hot water draw-off piping may be used for both units, the isolation of one system from the other being effected by the operation of one or more stopcocks or a two-way valve. The heater is not, however, suitable for operation as a booster and must therefore be supplied with cold water. Whichever cold and hot water systems of supply are adopted the expansion pipe must always remain open to the atmosphere, and to the hot water storage tank when the boiler is in use, but must be capable of isolation from the heater when the latter is in operation. An isolating stopcock ('B' in Fig. 23) must therefore be incorporated and a second stopcock ('A' in Fig. 23) is required to turn off the supply to the heater when the boiler is in use.

When it is proposed to fit a gas water heater as an alternative to a solid fuel heating system, a careful study of the existing plumbing should be made and the lay-out sketched accurately after all the pipes have been traced and their purpose determined.

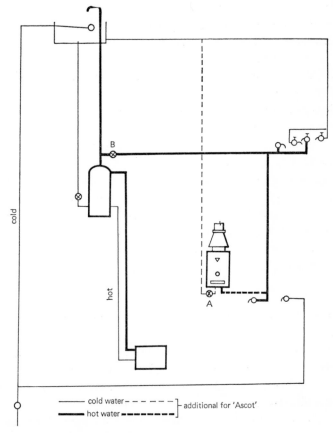

Fig. 23   Water heater as an auxiliary

WATER SUPPLY

The cold water supply to the heater should be taken from the cold water storage cistern in one of the following ways.

1.   By means of an independent supply pipe direct from the cistern to the heater.

2.   By teeing from the cold feed between the supply cistern and the cold water taps in the bathroom.

3.   By teeing off from the existing cold water supply pipe to the hot water tank, but at a point above the level of the top of this tank.

Where there is insufficient height from cistern supply, the heater may be connected direct to the incoming cold main provided the following conditions are observed.

(a) That permission of the Local Water Authority is obtained.

(b) That no connection is made between the outlet of the heater and any pipe connected to any tank. This necessitates the fitting of independent taps for the heater delivery.

Whichever system is employed, the existing expansion pipe must always remain open to atmosphere and to the hot tank or cylinder, but the draw-off pipe must be capable of isolation from the expansion pipe and from the whole boiler system.

The correct procedure for the change-over from one system to the other should be fully understood by the consumer, otherwise an incorrect sequence may be carried out, resulting in unsatisfactory operation of the heater when, for example, both stopcocks are left open.

SIMPLE BOILER SYSTEM FOR THE SUPPLY OF DOMESTIC HOT WATER

The incorporation of a multi-point heater to operate as an alternative to the existing system can be arranged by following the lay-out shown in Fig. 23 provided the hot water feed pipe from the boiler to the kitchen sink is 22 mm nominal bore:

1.   The heater is supplied direct with cold water via a 22 mm distributing pipe from the cold water supply tank.

2.　A stopcock 'A' of approved pattern is fitted to this pipe close to the inlet of the heater.

3.　The outlet of the heater is connected by a short length of 22 mm pipe to the 22 mm draw-off pipe from the boiler system, but close to the sink tap.

4.　A second cock 'B' is fitted to the boiler system draw-off pipe between the expansion pipe and the first branch, thus isolating all hot draw-off pipes from the boiler system when the heater is put into operation.

To change from Boiler to Heater:

1.　Close stopcock 'B'

2.　Open stopcock 'A'

To change from Heater to Boiler:

1.　Close stopcock 'A'

2.　Open stopcock 'B'

Alternatively the heater may be connected by adopting the following methods:

1.　The 22 mm cold water supply is taken from the cold feed to the hot cylinder at a point above the level of the top of the hot water tank.

2.　A stopcock 'A' of approved design is fitted close to the inlet of the heater.

The following alternative hot water draw-off should be utilized where the hot water feed pipe to the kitchen sink is 15 mm nominal bore.

1.　A separate 22 mm pipe is run from outlet of the heater to a second hot water tap at the sink.

2.　From this point a 22 mm hot water pipe is run to a two-way cock situated on the hot water draw-off pipe between the hot water tank and the nearest draw-off branch. Care must be taken to see that the two-way cock is fitted in such a way as to give the correct alternative paths.

Metric Units for Gas

The new metric units intended to replace imperial units in the gas industry, have been agreed between the Gas Council and the Department of Trade and Industry.

The units will not come into general use until the detailed changeover programme is agreed, and any necessary changes made in the legislation. Nevertheless, since there is interest in them outside the gas industry, they are being announced now to facilitate long term planning. Details of their general introduction will be announced in due course, though general use is unlikely before 1975.

The principal agreed metric units are shown below, beside the units they will replace. Their proper abbreviations are shown in brackets.

	Imperial unit	Metric unit
1. *Pressure*	inches water gauge (in.wg)	millibar (mbar)
	pounds per square inch (psi)	bar (bar)
2. *Standard reference conditions for gas volumes*		
Temperature	60° Fahrenheit (60°F)	15° Celsius (15°C)
Pressure	30 inches of mercury (30″Hg)	1013·25 mbar
Condition	saturated with water	dry
3. *Sales unit*	Therm	One hundred megajoules (100 MJ)
4. *Calorific value*	British Thermal Units per cubic foot (Btu/cu.ft)	megajoules per cubic metre (MJ/m³)
5. *Heat rate*	British Thermal Units per hour (Btu/hr)	kilowatt (kW) OR, where information may be required to calculate running costs, megajoules per hour will be given *in addition to* kilowatts—e.g. kW(MJ/h)

7 | Domestic Central Heating

The requirements of human beings vary considerably when it comes to personal comforts and they are influenced by age, sex, state of health, personal preferences and prejudices. The heating engineer must be guided by his customer in deciding the temperatures for the various parts of the house in which he is installing a central heating plant.

However, there are general guidelines and it is accepted by the heating trade that 21°C is a suitable temperature for the living room, 13 to 16°C for bedrooms, 16 to 18°C for bathroom and 16°C for most other areas of the house.

In trying to achieve comfort conditions to his customer's requirements, the heating engineer will take into account the type of house construction, its situation, local climatic conditions, the state of doors, windows and the roof within the house, because all these factors affect his recommendations in the matters of heating form and the appliances to be installed.

The engineer will make a careful survey of the house and from his findings and measurements he will make elaborate calculations. In these calculations he is mainly concerned with heat losses. In this matter, the wise householder will concern himself with insulation before he decides on the installation of any form of central heating. The golden rule is to keep the cold out of the house rather than warm it continuously once it has penetrated the holes, openings, cracks and surfaces. Half the cost of heating in most houses arises from poor or below standard insulation. Anyone who has installed a good double glazing system will understand this all important point.

The reputable heating engineer will be prepared to advise the householder, and from the results of his survey be able to discuss the best methods of heating the house. He will make recommendations on (1) full house heating by which every part of the house will be heated constantly to a specified temperature, (2) part house heating which, as the term implies, will give specific temperatures to selected rooms or parts of the house and (3) background heating by which the whole or part of the house is heated and the temperature maintained at a lower level, supplemented by local heat for bodily comfort.

There is a wide variety of choice today from which to select the type of heating installation to suit individual needs. There can be no 'cheap' installation and householders are advised to always seek the services of qualified installers. Beware of the door salesman and the man who is prepared to do the work in the evening or at the weekend. People have suffered a great deal from the unqualified charlatans who call themselves plumbers and heating engineers without any right to the titles.

Small Pipe Central Heating

In this chapter we concern ourselves with those forms of heating commonly known as 'smallbore' and 'microbore' (also known as 'minibore').

It is not possible in this book to cover the subject in detail because central heating in any form is a specialized subject and serious study is required if any plumber is intending to set himself up as an installer. The following is intended as a guide only and would-be designers and installers should read and digest the valuable technical literature obtainable from the British Standards Institution, Institution of Heating and Ventilating Engineers, Institute of Plumbing, British Gas Corporation, Electricity Council, Copper Development Association and others.

The original purpose of developing the smallbore heating system was to heat a dwelling of up to 140 m² floor area. It is nevertheless possible to install the system in premises having a much larger area, provided the installation can be designed round a centrally placed heating unit, making it possible to design the piping layout to include more but shorter pipe circuits.

Briefly, the smallbore heating system comprises a boiler to

which radiators are connected by means of small diameter tubes, and heated water being forced through the tubes and radiators by means of a specially designed pump or circulator.

To ensure proper temperature control, an automatically operated mixing valve is used in conjunction with a by-pass pipe. This mixing valve, which is actuated by the outside air temperature, thus ensures that the heat output from the radiators is controlled under such weather conditions, without affecting the boiler temperature. Such an arrangement ensures that adequate heat is available in the boiler to give an abundant and constant supply of domestic hot water.

DOMESTIC HOT WATER SUPPLY

On the domestic hot water side, it is essential to use an indirect copper cylinder coupled to the boiler by an independent gravity circuit. This circuit is normally run in 22 mm or 28 mm copper tubing and is entirely separate from the radiator runs, apart from the permissible case of a towel rail being fitted.

The purpose of using an indirect cylinder is that it will act as an accumulator to absorb any excess heat in the boiler, in the event of a sudden reduction in the required heating load and until the boiler damper control slows down the burning rate.

Returning to the heating side of the installation, it is generally only necessary to use 15 mm diameter copper tubes in the heating circuits apart from where the circuits run into a common flow and return. At such points these common mains would be increased to 22 mm.

The use of small diameter copper tubes in the heating mains means that there is no need to hide them from view, as they are neat in appearance and can be run so as to blend with the surroundings. The pump allows great freedom in deciding pipe runs, thus permitting easy installation without costly structural work or damage to interior decorations. Furthermore, a considerable saving in pipe length is achieved because it is not necessary to rise above the floor levels on which the radiators are to be fitted;

this, in turn, results in lower heat losses from the distribution system and a consequent saving in fuel.

The pipe runs need not be laid with a constant rise or fall for ventilating purposes. Inverted loop circuits, such as may be met with in running round the door casings, may be used, without fear of air-locking the system. Air-cocks fitted at such points are used only during the initial filling up of the installation. Generally, single pipe circuits connecting two or more radiators are used, the temperature difference between the flow and return being of the order of 11°C. With such a low differential the radiators are all maintained at more or less the same temperature. Obviously, the number of circuits used in any given installation will vary according to the type of dwelling involved, the positioning of the rooms and whether it is a house or bungalow. In general, the normal house would have two, or at the most three, major pipe circuits with perhaps a short loop feeding a single radiator as might be required in a hall or cloakroom.

To ensure that the full benefit of a smallbore heating system is obtained, it is advisable to insulate the roof space so as to avoid loss of heat and consequent waste of fuel. The domestic hot water storage cylinder should be fitted with an insulating jacket and where, as in the case of a bungalow, any pipes are run in the roof space, they must be protected against heat loss.

Design

In designing a smallbore heating installation the following procedure should be adopted:

1. Decide the required room temperature and then calculate the heat losses through walls, floors, ceilings, etc.
2. Plan radiator positions and pipe runs.
3. Calculate the friction losses in pipe circuits, and determine from these the pump size.
4. Size the radiators and boiler.

Room temperature requirements may vary from client to client, but generally the room temperatures recommended in British Standard Code of Practice CP 3006, Part 1: 1969 will find ready acceptance. Thus the following temperatures can be taken as giving comfort conditions:

21°C for living-rooms.

13°C for bedrooms.

16°C for hall and staircase.

Where a room is used only intermittently and for comparatively short periods, such as a dining-room, it is advisable to adopt a design temperature of 21°C, thus ensuring a quicker warming-up of the room concerned. Generally with ordinary domestic premises there is sufficient heat available in the kitchen from the boiler itself and the various hot water pipe mains and flue pipes to maintain an adequate temperature. Where an outside boiler is used provision must be made to warm the kitchen and in this case 18°C will be found to be a satisfactory temperature.

The foregoing temperatures are those required to give full central heating comfort. Where, however, open fires are to be used with the smallbore heating system providing only background heating, 16°C may be taken as the design temperature for living-rooms. With the room temperatures decided, the heat requirements can now be calculated, starting off by taking the difference between outside and selected inside temperatures to give the temperature difference rise, the outside temperature always being taken as 1°C.

The heat loss through walls, ceilings, floors and windows is then dealt with. The amount of heat lost through these surfaces is known as thermal transmission, which in turn can be defined as the amount of heat in watts (W) which will flow through 1 m^2 of a particular type and thickness of construction when the temperatures of the air adjoining the inner and outer faces differ by 1°C. This is called the 'U value' and for the convenience of the heating designer, complete tables giving the U values for most forms of construction are available in table form from the British Standards Institution and Institution of Heating and Ventilating Engineers.

The formula for calculating heat transmission through a structure is $H = U(ti - to) \times A$, where H is the heat transmission, U the transmission coefficient of the structure, W/m²°C, ti is the inside air temperature, to is the outside air temperature and A is the area of the structure.

Air changes must be allowed for when calculating heat losses and this applies particularly to rooms with large open fireplaces, which will withdraw air at least three times that necessary for normal ventilation purposes. In houses having central heating it will be found that the room temperature will drop several degrees when an open fire is lit. The use of a modern fireplace with an adjustable restrictive flue throat can keep the flow of air to chimney to a minimum in such circumstances.

In the case of 'open plan' types of houses it is generally necessary to assume a room temperature of 21°C and maintain this for calculation purposes throughout the whole house.

Having completed the calculations for each room they are added together to give the total heat losses throughout the house. The total is defined in watts.

The next step is to plan the radiator positions and pipe runs. This is a matter that requires some care. Wherever possible, radiators should be sited under windows. The advantages gained thereby are as follows:

They make use of all areas not normally occupied.

They avoid the soiling of decorations by dust-laden convection currents.

They overcome down-draught.

They provide better temperature distribution through the room.

In some cases, particularly in existing premises, built-in furniture may make siting of radiators under a window impossible, and they may have to be mounted on or against a full wall. Under these conditions, one should always fit a canopy across the full length of the radiator top to prevent staining of the walls and ceilings by dust-laden convection currents.

In preparing a plan of the pipe runs, it should always be borne in mind that the shorter the pipe circuit the better. The plan itself should be drawn to a sufficiently large scale for all pipe runs, with the positions of valves clearly indicated. Later as each pipe circuit is sized, the pipe diameter should be marked on the drawing. If an isometric projection is drawn, quantities may be read off from it.

FRICTION LOSSES

With the pipe circuit, radiators and valves marked on the drawing, the next step is to calculate the friction losses through the pipe runs, to ensure that they come within the pressure head range of the available and suitable types of pumps. It is here that the choice of copper tube, as a suitable material to use, becomes a major factor. The smooth internal surface, allied to a slightly larger bore than the equivalent iron tube, gives a much lower friction factor. Further, as the manufacturing tolerances for copper tubes are much less than is the case with iron pipes, greater accuracy is obtained in calculating friction losses. Added to this, the copper tube has a slightly smaller outside diameter, making for neater appearance.

To arrive at the friction losses in the pipe circuits, these are each measured separately to give the actual length of pipe in each circuit, to which is added an allowance of one-third to cover the frictional resistance of fittings and valves, etc. While this may seem an arbitrary method to adopt it is indeed one that has been found to give very satisfactory results.

HEATING LOAD

The heating load will be taken by the radiators and it will be equal to the total heat losses, less the heat emitted from exposed pipework in the various rooms. Tables are available to enable calculations to be made of the heat emission from runs of pipe of differing diameters but broadly speaking, emission from pipe and radiator surfaces depends on the difference between the mean temperature of the water in the system, and the room temperature. In forced circulation systems the temperature drop will be between $11°C$ and $16°C$ and this differential affects pipe sizing insofar that it determines the rate of water circulation and consequently, the frictional resistance of the circuit.

By adopting the higher differential of 16°C the water circulation will be lowered thereby reducing friction. On the other hand, this differential means a lower difference between the water temperature in the system and the room temperature, and this could call for larger radiators in certain rooms and the possible need of 22 mm connections. For this reason the 11°C is generally adopted for smallbore systems. This lower differential ensures that the radiators at the extreme ends of the circuit will receive water at higher temperatures, and also allows a rapid heating up of the system from cold.

Frictional resistance is an important factor in pumped circulations and in the event of the resistance of a circuit being greater than the available circulating head, the circuit must be re-designed to give a smaller total length. Alternatively, the designer can re-group the radiators to give an additional circuit, thus spreading the heating load. As already mentioned it might be advisable to increase the pipe size to 22 mm for part of the main circuit. On the other hand, the higher differential of 16°C might solve the problem because the effect of this would be to lessen the frictional resistance in the main circuit.

Where two or more circuits share common flow and return mains, the heating loads of the circuits served must be calculated and used to obtain the resistance of the common mains from the graph. Equally, the heating load of the common mains, by emission and any radiators they feed, must be divided proportionately between the circuits they serve.

The short connecting mains between the various radiator circuits and boiler are usually 22 mm tubes, except where there are four or more separate radiator circuits; in these instances, a 28 mm diameter tube should be used.

SIZE OF RADIATORS

Finally, it is necessary to calculate the radiator surface area that each room requires and to choose the type most suitable for the purpose. To calculate the radiator surface for any room, first take the actual metre run of exposed pipe in that room and multiply this length by the emission factor. This figure is then subtracted from the total heat requirement of the room, which had previously been found. The remainder is divided by the radiator transmission factor for an average temperature difference between the water in the radiator and the ambient air, to give the total radiator surface required.

With the normal cast iron or steel radiators, an average transmission factor of 23·8 W/m°C may be accepted. Working with this factor and knowing the length of exposed pipe in the room, the required radiator area for a room with a heat loss of 2·344 kW and having 6·09 m run of exposed pipe, 40 square feet of radiator surface would suffice.

Generally, the choice of the particular type of radiator used is a matter for consultation with the householder. Panel wall radiators are very popular if there is enough space available to accommodate the required length. Where space is very limited, the cast iron column radiator, with its high heat transmission, may have to be fitted despite its somewhat ugly appearance.

SIZE OF BOILER

There is now only the boiler to consider. Whether it be gas fired, oil or solid-fuel burning depends on the householder's preference but it must be capable of meeting the maximum demand likely to be imposed by the heating system, plus an adequate margin to cover the needs of the domestic hot water supply. A minimum of 3·517 kW should be allowed for this latter, over and above the total central heating needs. The boiler must be fitted with a thermostat that is reliable in action, to ensure good control of the burning rate. It is recommended that the boiler manufacturer be consulted regarding any particular appliances.

Since the introduction of smallbore heating, a number of boiler manufacturers have devoted considerable attention to reducing the running costs of heating systems. The result is that today there are excellent clock-controlled boilers that are designed to operate separate circuits for day or night only as required. This is achieved by having two separate flow connections, one running to the bedrooms or night areas, and the other to the living rooms or day areas. By pre-setting the separate clocks on each of these circuits they are automatically switched on or off, thus providing heat in the required places at the appropriate times. The result is that with such installations a much smaller boiler is used and it therefore operates at a constant and high efficiency. As a case in point, where under ordinary conditions a boiler of 13·19 kW would be necessary, a clock-controlled boiler of 9·68 kW only would be called for.

PUMP AND CONTROL EQUIPMENT

Smallbore copper tube forced circulating heating systems can only work if the correct type of pump is used. There are a number of suitable makes available, and all of these are of the 'canned rotor' type, without glands between the motor and the impeller. The advantages of this form of construction are: (1) no possibility of water leaking out, and (2) as the bearings are water lubricated, no periodical oiling or greasing is necessary. The electric motor itself is of the squirrel cage induction type having a power consumption of approximately 70 watts, and both the motor and the impeller are, to all intents and purposes, silent in operation. This is an important consideration where the pump may be working at night, when even the slightest noise can be a constant source of annoyance. The maximum size of pump available at the moment is one of 37·36 mbar and with this particular pump 12 mm diameter copper tubes have been used successfully for the heating pipe circuit.

Circulator

The circulator should, whenever possible, be installed in the return main. The reason for this is that it is then operating at a lower temperature than would be the case if it were fitted into the flow pipe and can, if need be, have cork blocks mounted underneath as a stand and to prevent vibration. With installations having heating mains at a level below that of the expansion tank which is less than the pressure head developed by the circulator, it should be fitted in the flow-pipe to avoid the likelihood of sub-atmo-spheric pressures in the high-level mains. Such conditions may sometimes be encountered in fitting heating installations in bunga-lows, where the pipe circuits may be run at or near ceiling level.

It is important to note that, because of the close fit between the impeller and the case, all parts of the installation should be thoroughly cleaned and flushed out to remove any swarf or other foreign matter likely to jam the pump or cause damage to the bearings.

Electrical Starting Gear

In dealing with the electrical starting gear, it is imperative that the push-button starter recommended and supplied by the pump manufacturers should be used. This is fitted with the correct current overload release to protect the field coils of the motor from possible damage by over-heating or burning out in the event of the impeller becoming jammed.

Control Equipment

With a smallbore heating system using only a small amount of water working under forced circulation, a very large degree of flexibility is available. Because of this, individual radiators may be turned on or off to suit any given requirements. With the small amount of water used, and that under pressure, there is no long waiting period between turning on any radiator and that radiator reaching the correct operating temperature. However, it is desirable that some method of controlling the entire system in relation to the outside air temperatures should be fitted to every smallbore heating installation. Such form of control will ensure economic running of the system and at the same time provide a constant and adequate supply of domestic hot water. It may be thought that control by the boiler thermostat alone would be a satisfactory method to adopt. It cannot be emphasized too strongly that such a practice must be avoided, because if such control were used, the closing down of the boiler firing rate would equally cut the heat output to the domestic water side.

CONTROL METHODS

The ideal method of control is one that is fully automatic and works through a temperature-sensitive bulb fitted outside the house. A capillary tube runs from the bulb to a three-way control valve fitted to the flow-pipe from the boiler and a by-pass connecting it to the main return pipe. The temperature-sensitive element, being continuously in operation, opens or closes the mixing valve on the heating mains conversely with the outside temperature and thus maintains, within limits, the room temperature at a constant figure. The motive power to operate the control comes from the pressure differential across the pump. By using this type of control unit, all rooms are maintained at the correct temperature and localized air disturbances caused by open doors and windows in some rooms do not affect other rooms. The small additional cost of this piece of equipment should, it is claimed, be recouped over two or three heating seasons by reason of the expected saving in fuel costs.

An alternative method of control is to use room thermostats coupled to the pump, thereby controlling the amount of heat passed to the radiators. There are, however, a number of disadvantages attached to this, such as finding suitable positions for mounting and the cost of installing the necessary switch and electric mains wiring. Similarly, individual radiator thermostatic control would be expensive and would leave the heating mains 'alive' with a consequent waste of fuel.

The only other way of dealing with the problem is to install a three-way by-pass valve connected between flow and return mains, and to adjust the valve manually. This entails the householder altering the setting to meet outside temperature variations.

A variation of the three-way by-pass valve is also available. It consists of an automatic three-way mixing valve, with a bimetal spiral in the upper part of the valve casing, controlling the movement of the double clack in the lower part, which either opens the inlet port or closes the return port, so that a mixed flow temperature can be selected and maintained.

ISOLATING VALVES

It is advisable to provide an isolating valve on both the flow and return mains. This will allow the radiators and pipe circuits to be drained without shutting down the boiler and domestic hot water supply side of the system. The valve on the flow main only may be closed in the event of wishing to shut down the central heating circuits. If the valve on the return were closed, there would be a likelihood of high pressure occurring in the heating system due to the expansion of water.

Lock shield valves should be mounted on the return main of all secondary circuits; this will enable the circulation to be reduced to the required rate and will also prevent 'short-circuiting' of the major circuits. The adjustment of the lock shield valves on the secondary circuits is carried out when the system is first put into use, so that with all the radiators working, the water in the return mains from all circuits is at the same temperature.

Installation

The technique of installing smallbore copper tubes is a matter with which plumbers and heating engineers are familiar as part of their normal work. Copper tubing used for a heating installation is dealt with in the same way. It must, however, be realized that with a smallbore heating installation, most of the pipes are run on wall surfaces and are plainly visible. Under such conditions, the installing of pipe runs and fittings must be done in the neatest manner, so that the completed job is unobtrusive and harmonizes with the surrounding decorations. In a new house, it is preferable that the pipework should be done after plastering has been finished, but prior to the completion of the painting and decorating.

It is because of this need for neatness that light gauge copper tubes are so suitable. Copper pipes do not rust and painting is unnecessary. In addition, the ductility of the metal allows it to be manipulated with ease, whilst the strength of light gauge copper tube is more than adequate for the service it has to perform.

The smooth internal surfaces are important because of the low frictional resistance they offer to the flow of water.

From the decorative point of view, the smooth non-rusting external surfaces have much to commend them; they can be polished easily and readily take a plated finish, features that can be exploited to fit in with the surrounding decorative treatment.

JOINTS

The jointing of the copper tubes may be carried out with either capillary soldered fittings or compression fittings.

In general, the type of joint chosen must not in any way restrict the bore of the tube, and in addition should preferably be so fixed to allow for easy dismantling. This last point is of particular importance where it may be necessary to provide additional circuits or radiators at a later date. It has been found that many people, when having central heating installed, try to save money by cutting down the number of radiators initially installed. In such cases, provision for the additional circuits can always be made by inserting tee-pieces at the required points and blanking off the branches.

CLIPS

The stand-off type of clip should always be used and spaced at intervals of not more than 1·25 m. This type of clip holds the pipe off the wall approximately 0·10 mm and thereby prevents possible damage of paintwork by overheating. It allows easy cleaning of the pipes and gives sufficient room for painting the surface behind them.

Where inverted pipe loops are formed in passing over doorways and similar obstructions, experience has shown that it is not necessary to fit open vents at these points. Ventcocks should be fitted on any loop or circuit that cannot be cleared of air through the radiators, for use when first filling up the system. In the same way, draincocks should be fitted in the return main near to the boiler and also on any circuit run at a level below that of the boiler.

EXPANSION CISTERN

As with every other hot water heating system, a separate expansion cistern must be fitted from which cold water feed is taken and connected into the return main close to the boiler. The cold water feed-pipe should be connected to the bottom of the heating return main by means of a 'U' bend, or taken in at the side. The by-pass connections should be made with swept tees. Expansion pipes should not be smaller than 22 mm diameter.

TYPES OF RADIATORS

The type of radiator is a matter of individual preference. Consistent with its having the required heating surface, one or other of the many types of the wall, free standing, skirting panel or floorline patterns can be used.

Wall radiators should be mounted above the skirting and have at least 127 mm between the centre line and the bottom tappings and the heating main. It must be remembered that if the radiator is fixed too high on the wall, a higher temperature gradient between floor and ceiling will occur. Connections to the radiators may be made to the bottom tappings, but if this is done then a blind nipple must be inserted between the first and second sections at the bottom, to give an equal distribution of hot water within the radiator. Alternatively, the top flow and bottom return method of connection may be used. The usual angle valve must be fitted to each radiator, and may be on either flow or return as a matter of convenience, the second connection consisting of an ordinary bent male iron-to-copper union. In designing an installation, the use of radiators with heat emission greater than 2·05 kW should if possible, be avoided. Two small radiators to give the required heating surface would be better, otherwise with a large radiator the inlet and outlet connections may have to be increased in size to 22 mm.

SKIRTING HEATING PANELS

If it is desired to use skirting heating panels, care must be taken to see that the connections are fitted in such a way that by turning off the heat it does not interfere with the flow of hot water to heating units in other rooms. Heat emission data for skirting heating, convector heaters or similar units must be obtained from the manufacturers.

Where a pipe has to pass through a wall or ceiling a 28 mm copper or brass sleeve should be fitted after drilling the hole in the required position. Powered angle drills are available which enable clean neat holes to be drilled close in to the corner.

CONNECTIONS TO THE BOILER

In connecting the return main to the boiler, it is essential that the stream of water returning under pressure is not injected into the return pipe of the domestic hot water system. This could give rise to reverse circulation to the indirect cylinder. If there is only one return tapping on the boiler, a twin elbow or pitcher tee should be used and the lead to the heating main reduced to the required pipe size. Where it is more convenient to take both the heating and domestic flow mains from a single boiler tapping, a 35 mm pitcher tee with a reduced branch should be used to ensure an adequate supply to the gravity circulating primary side of the hot water storage cylinder.

THERMOMETERS

Thermometers should be fitted, one on the boiler and a second in the flow-pipe past the by-pass and control valve. The latter will give the temperature of the water going to the radiators as distinct from the boiler water.

FLUSHING

Finally, before the completed installation is put into service the whole system, boiler, pipework, cistern and radiators, must be thoroughly flushed out at least three times to ensure removal of swarf, filings and any dirt that may be present. This is a most important factor in ensuring a fully successful and trouble-free heating system. In this connection it must also be remembered how necessary it is to remove cutting burrs when the tube has been cut to the required lengths.

If, as in the case of cast-iron radiators, it is necessary to paint them, it should be remembered that metallic paints reduce the heat transmission by approximately 15 per cent. With ordinary paints or enamels the efficiency is not affected.

Micro and Minibore Heating

Following development work during the late 1960s the Wednesbury Tube Company introduced their 'Microbore' system in 1968. The Copper Development Association had published details of the system known as 'Minibore' in 1967 and many hundreds of these systems were installed and those in service are said to have fully justified the claims made in the early stages, proving them to be efficient and economical both in materials and labour.

The basic principles of Microbore and Minibore heating follow closely those of a standard smallbore heating system. In fact, the principles and practices laid down in the Standard Code of Practice for smallbore central heating installation should be followed.

There are two basic systems of this development in small pipe heating, (1) open tank (see Fig. 24A) and (2) sealed tank (Fig. 24B).

The low pressure system is the most frequently installed of the two, although the pressurized system is becoming recognized now because of the higher temperatures that can be achieved using smaller heating units. Both systems employ 8 mm or 10 mm tubes on the radiator circuits and these are connected to flow and return manifolds formed in 22 mm or 28 mm copper tube. It is advantageous in a bungalow to connect all the radiators to a single pair of manifolds located close to the boiler. In a house of one or more storeys it will be more convenient to install a pair of manifolds on each floor, siting them in the most central and accessible position so that the length of the 8 mm diameter copper circuits to the radiators can be kept short to save material and reduce frictional resistance to a minimum.

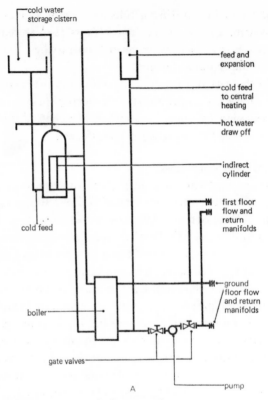

Fig. 24   A Layout for a typical open-tank system

It cannot be emphasized too strongly that all calculations for microbore (the term most widely used now) must be determined correctly because the design for this system is more critical than for smallbore.

The advantages of microbore can be summarized as follows:

(a) The installation time is reduced providing a cost saving.

(b) The disturbance of a household is confined to a minimum during installation.

(c) A reduction in the cost of materials used.

(d) A more flexible installation which permits extension at a later date.

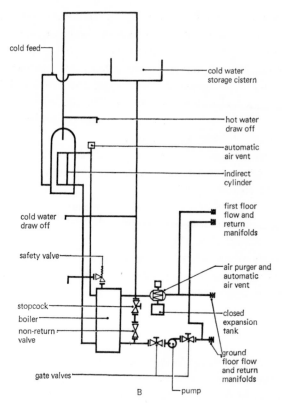

B Layout for a typical sealed-tank system

(e) A reduced water content which provides more sensitivity to thermostatic control.

(f) A faster heat recovery is achieved.

DESIGN AND INSTALLATION OF MICROBORE

Copper tubing for microbore installations is manufactured to BS 2871, Part 2 and it is available in 6 mm, 8 mm and 10 mm outside diameter. The tube is supplied in coil lengths of 10 m, 20 m, 25 m, 30 m and 50 m and it is of soft temper which permits easy manipulation by hand, or pipe-bending springs if sharp radius bends are required. The soft-temper tube reduces the noise level in the system which occurs with high velocities.

The manifold could be described as the heart of the microbore system. There are a number of patterns available one of which is called the 'Microfold' manufactured by the Wednesbury Tube Company. This component is fabricated from a length of copper tube with a disc brazed in the centre, thereby providing both flow and return chambers in one unit. To this length a number of stub bosses is soldered which have compression fittings to which the microbore tubing is connected.

Three patterns of Microfold are available:
WM18 designed for use with up to nine radiators and a maximum capacity of 26 kW
WM12 for up to six radiators and a maximum of 17 kW
WM8 constructed of 22 mm copper tube having provision for up to four radiators of 11 kW

The ends of the Microfold are to half-hard temper to allow the use of compression or capillary fittings. A special spanner is supplied to fit easily between the stub bosses when making connections.

DOUBLE ENTRY RADIATOR VALVE

The double entry radiator valve is intended to complete the termination of the twin microbore tubes at one tapping on the radiator, making a neat unobtrusive connection. The valve has a BSP taper thread which screws into the radiator. The twin outlets are designed to take 10 mm tube.

During the installation it should be noted that the flow connection is nearer to the radiator and the return is into the valve body. In operation the valve controls the return from the radiator.

When using this valve with standard single panel radiators a length of 10 mm tube is fitted to the valve and inserted into the bottom waterway of the radiator for return circulation. The length of this tube should not be less than 180 mm. In the case of double panel radiators, a special flexible insert is necessary to negotiate the header of the radiator. This flexible insert must be used in all double panel radiators.

When fitting microbore tubing, a length a little more than the distance between the manifold and the radiator is uncoiled and then cut with pliers to ensure that the ends of the pipe are closed together to prevent the ingress of extraneous matter. When preparing the pipe for jointing it must be cut with a fine-toothed hacksaw and the burrs removed with a fine file.

As already stated, the nature of the copper tube facilitates the bending and fixing of microbore. New methods of pipe clipping are being used and a number of clips and cover strips are available. It is sufficient however to restrict the clips to parts where the tube is exposed and needs to be secured down the side of window frames or along the skirting board. The cover strip gives the neatest finish to tubes prominently in view. The flow and return pipes can often be installed without disturbing the normal working of the house, a fact very much appreciated by the householder.

In new houses, a plastic coated microbore tube can be buried in the plaster, eliminating the need for other protective measures. Care must always be exercised in running out the coil of tubing to protect it from sharp edges which could kink the tube and affect the performance of the heating circuit.

On completion of the installation, the whole system should be washed out immediately to ensure that no foreign bodies remain in the tubes. Some form of inhibitor should be added when recharging the system.

Sealed Systems

All wet heating systems are operated by the continuous recycling of water by means of a pump through the boiler and radiators or unit heaters, and it is of paramount importance that only minimum water replacement should take place. However, following the principle of the Perkins system, engineers in America and on the Continent have, for many years, been using a sealed-tank method by which loss of water from the system is virtually eliminated. There is therefore little need for periodic 'topping up' and a mains supply through a ball valve is not required.

SEALED EXPANSION TANK

In a closed system it is essential to install, at a convenient point in the circuit, a sealed expansion tank (sometimes called a flexible membrane vessel) which is just large enough to take up the expansion volume when the temperature rises (see Fig. 25). The vessel is normally of a welded steel construction into which is fitted a flexible diaphragm dividing it into two compartments, one of which is filled with nitrogen or air, and the other with water from the heating system: the absorption of air into the water— which occurred with the Perkins system—is thereby prevented. The air or nitrogen cushion is pressurized to support the static head created by the height of the water in the system so that the original gas volume remains unchanged when the system is filled up. When the boiler is fired and the water temperature rises, expansion of the water pushes back the diaphragm and compresses the nitrogen or air on the opposite side, causing an increase of pressure throughout the system.

With all sealed systems, the optimum size for the vessel is dependent upon the water capacity and the working temperature of the installation. A range of flexible membrane vessels is available and the manufacturers should be consulted regarding selection.

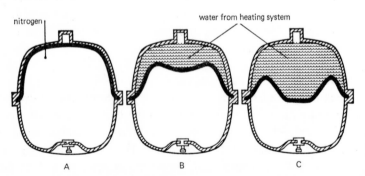

Fig. 25   Expansion tank with flexible diaphragm for sealed system. (A) Before the boiler has been fired the tank contains only air or nitrogen. (B) As the temperature rises the diaphragm moves to accept the increased water volume. (C) Position of diaphragm when water temperature has reached its maximum.

Location of Sealed Expansion Tank

As the sealed expansion tank is comparatively small, it can be placed at more or less any convenient point in the system, and this obviously makes concealment relatively easy. Where there is a possibility of tanks being isolated when valves are shut off many installers position the expansion tank close to the boiler. If an air purger fitting, which consists of a simple air separation and float-type air vent, is used, venting can, if required, be a semi-automatic operation. Installation costs can be reduced by fitting a combined sealed tank and air purger unit. If the layout of the pipework is such as to make it more convenient for the sealed tank and air purger units to be installed separately, this will not impair the efficiency of the system, but it is recommended that

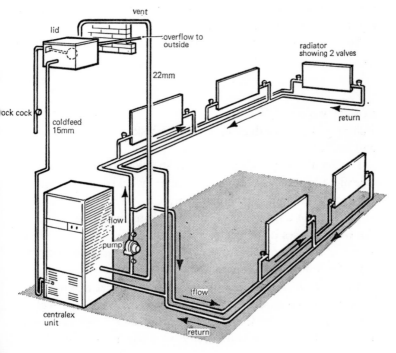

g. 26   The Centralec system of heating

the air purger should be at the point of highest temperature and therefore as close to the boiler as possible. To gain full economic advantage from the sealed system the average water temperature should generally be higher than for the open-tank system. However, there are many sealed-tank installations in use working at a mean temperature of 78°C, the average for open-tank systems.

The Centralec System of Heating

Centralec is an electric heat generator using mainly off peak electricity. It is designed to be connected to either small or microbore conventional hot water radiators and/or fan convectors. It has no flue, no flames, no smells, no fumes. It produces no ash, no dust, no mess. It needs no vents for combustion of air. It needs the very minimum of maintenance—has no burner system needing regular cleaning and its efficiency is constant.

The Centralec system is shown in diagrammatical form in Fig. 26.

HOW IT WORKS

Figure 27 shows in diagram a cross-section of the heat generator and exchanger.

During the night charge period the flow boiler provides the overnight heat requirements. The fan is switched off thus allowing the core to attain its maximum charge.

During the day heat is withdrawn from the storage core by a fan which passes it across an air/water heat exchanger. The heated water is then pumped out to the radiator system at a thermostatically controlled temperature.

Centralec is so designed to use a proportional amount of day time energy—provided by the flow boiler. This energy will only be required during the colder weather and is provided automatically by the flow boiler being switched into circuit so as to maintain the required flow temperature.

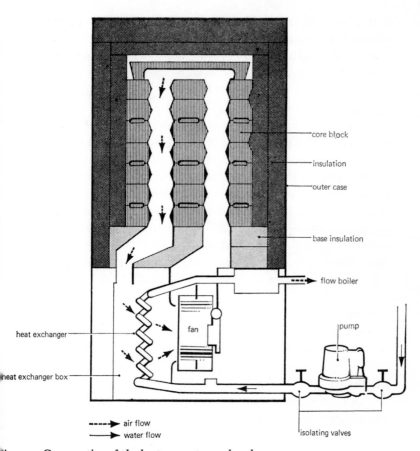

Fig. 27   Cross-section of the heat generator and exchanger

The System

The system may be either smallbore or microbore with a circulating pump suited to whichever system is used. The radiator system is similar in operation to any other.

Hot Water

In a home with Centralec, hot water for baths is supplied in the normal way by a hot water cylinder and immersion heater system.

The Centralec store is thus reserved for space heating and is independent of the domestic hot water system. This avoids the problem of running the boiler at low efficiency and possible discomfort in summer time to provide hot water only, as with some fuel-fired systems.

Control

Temperature in the dwelling can be controlled by a room thermostat which will interrupt the fan circuit and thus stop the flow of hot air across the heat exchanger.

Alternatively, thermostatic radiator valves may be used to give individual room temperature control providing a byepass loop is fitted in the system. Centralec has been designed to operate throughout the 24 hours of the day. The room thermostat should therefore not be switched off during the 8 hour charge period. Any reduction in night heating will increase the percentage of day rate energy usage.

Temperatures

When the storage core is fully charged, the case temperature of the unit will not exceed 86°C rise.

Dimensions

The box dimensions of present designs are 610 × 610 mm. Height varies between 1,225 and 1,625 mm depending on rated capacity and make.

Weight and Floor Loadings

The weight of a Centralec unit varies between 490 and 794 kg.

Therefore, the floor loadings are between 1,320 kg/m² and 2,140 kg/m².

DESIGN CONSIDERATIONS

Size and weight are the only two factors affecting the design of a building, and the location of the unit within the building. Because Centralec does not need air for combustion, it needs no primary air intake. It needs no flue and therefore, does not have to be located at the perimeter wall. Also the building design is not subject to the usual limitations of flues or chimneys.

Centralec is designed to emit a small amount of warmth continuously from its case, keeping the chill off the rooms and reducing the likelihood of condensation. To use this effect to the full, the unit is best located in a central position. Because it needs no flue, it may be sited virtually anywhere—under the stairs, in the kitchen or in a cupboard. A cellar would be ideal if there is one.

When the unit is in a cupboard, warm air from the case must be allowed to circulate freely through vents in the cupboard door also assisting the heating of the premises.

8 | Plumbing Fitments in the Home

The Kitchen

SINKS

The kitchen sink, from the days when it was made from brown earthenware and about three inches in depth, has now become an attractive as well as functional piece of kitchen equipment manufactured in a number of materials and designs.

Fireclay

There are several types of kitchen sink. The once popular 'Belfast' sink, which is made of fireclay and enamelled after baking, is still used in certain areas. It is easily fixed on brackets built into the wall, or on leg supports. This sink has a combined overflow, and a draining board can be made of the same material if required.

Stainless Steel

By far the most popular is the stainless steel sink and draining board combined, made in various sizes to suit individual requirements. The sink is stamped out of one sheet of metal, is very easy to keep clean and lends itself for use with purpose-made cabinets, giving a small streamlined finish (see Fig. 28A).

A double-compartment sink with double drainer is made for the larger kitchen, and this is becoming increasingly popular because it enables the housewife to prepare vegetables and, where necessary to keep them in soak in one compartment while the other can be used for washing the glass, china, cooking utensils, etc. One of this type is illustrated in Fig. 28B. The sinks and draining boards have a sound-deadening under-skin, and a food waste-grinding machine can also be attached. Another modern advantage is that some stainless steel sinks are made smaller and round in shape, so that no washing-up bowl is needed.

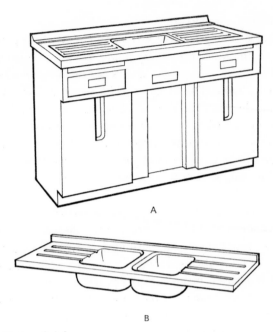

A

B

Fig. 28 *Types of sinks*
A Stainless steel sink unit
B Double compartment sink

In some cases the back skirting of the sink is pierced to enable the hot and cold services to be run along inside a cupboard and up through the skirting, finishing with a neat chromium-plated standard and whatever type of taps that may be desired, thus giving a very clean-looking finish.

Enamelled Steel
Another type is the vitreous enamelled steel sink. This is stamped out of one sheet of metal and after colour is applied, the sink is subjected to heat treatment giving the finished product a hard vitreous surface. These sinks can be obtained in various colours and sizes and, to provide the housewife with a complete unit, very attractive cabinets have been designed to match the varying colours of the sinks.

FOOD WASTE DISPOSERS

In the course of a year over a thousand meals (per person) are prepared in the kitchen of every home, not counting snacks and in-betweens. There is nearly always some form of waste from every type of food. This is either collected in a sink tidy or put into the bin beneath the sink to be taken out to the dustbin (in all weathers). Actually, it is a source of wonderment to many that while so much attention is being focused on germ protection in the storage and handling of food, decaying garbage lies in dustbins for days on end, attracting flies, wasps, rodents, stray dogs and cats!

There is no doubt at all that modern housewives are anxious to improve conditions in the kitchen and the disposal of food waste is, to some, a particularly nauseating job, i.e. cleaning scraps of food from the sink outlet, scooping peelings from the bowl, scraping congealed food from plates into the pedal bin, etc.

Engineers have designed a food waste disposer (Fig. 29A and B) which can be attached to the kitchen sink which will deal adequately with all forms of food waste.

The Scope of the Food Waste Disposer

The modern food waste disposer is an electro-mechanical device appended to the sink for the elimination of food waste, etc. These machines will dispose of all grades of food waste such as fish remains, fruit skins (including banana skins), vegetable parings, plate waste (including fatty materials), bones, eggshells and tea-leaves. Plastic materials, leather, rubber and fabrics are not readily disposable, but will do no electrical or mechanical damage to the device. It is not intended, of course, for the disposal of such articles nor for metals or string. Should any of these inadvertently slip into the machine they will do it no harm, but may cause the motor to stall and cut out the overload switch which protects the motor. The construction of the machine is usually so robust that they will not do it any mechanical damage. While any of these materials are in the grinding chamber they may be the cause of harsh noises from the machine. In the interests of smooth running, therefore, it is better to try and keep them out altogether. Glass and crockery are readily crushed by the machine and passed into the sewage system, but this practice should be avoided to prevent causing obstruction in the drains.

Installation
The food waste disposer has a 76 mm opening to the grinding chamber. This entails a 90 mm opening in the sink. Many sinks are now made with this size of opening to take either a food waste disposer or a crumb strainer waste. It is wise, therefore, if installing a new sink to see that it is one with a 90 mm opening.

Fireclay porcelain sinks of various types are now in production with and without overflows to take the food waste disposer.

If a stainless steel sink is already installed, it can usually be modified to take a disposer. The manufacturer of food waste disposers will lend plumbing contractors the necessary equipment to enlarge the hole and impress in it the recess for the disposer outlet. This is a simple operation for an experienced plumber.

Plumbing
This must be done in accordance with the Bye-laws of the area in which the installation is made. A trap must be inserted between the disposer and the drain. The discharge pipe from the machine should pass below the soil grid—this will prevent any objectionable build-up of waste on the grid.

The tail piece from the machine is copper pipe to which can be fixed any suitable type of trap. The minimum angle of the tail pipe should be $7\frac{1}{2}$ degrees—this will enable the well of the disposer to drain after use. The best position, however, for this tail piece is vertically downwards.

For ease of installation it is advisable to have the waste pipe outlet accessible, i.e. on one side or the other—not to the wall side of the unit.

When the disposer is being installed in a new house a side inlet gulley is the ideal fitment for the discharge.

It is most important that the waste pipe should not impose any

strain on the free hanging position of the disposer. This will tend
to make it noisy in operation.

All bends in the waste pipe system should be of generous radius
and formed without any distortion of the pipe bore.

Electrical

The motor incorporated in the disposer is designed to give the
maximum power from a 13 A fused plug. The rating of the motor
is over $\frac{1}{4}$ h.p. and is capable of a higher output over a short period.
The control of the unit should be of such a nature that it conforms
to I.E.E. requirements.

When running under the full load the motor takes 2·7 A, but
in the event of the motor stalling under overload conditions the
current taken by the motor will rise to 13 A. The circuit should
therefore be fused for this current. This current will only flow for
a few seconds until the overload device in the motor cuts it off.
The overload protection device is a red button situated at the
bottom of the motor on the waste outlet side. It is reset by pressing
it firmly upwards and it will re-engage with a slight click.

The reversing feature of the appliance (if specified) is the switch
below the point of the cable entry. This switch reverses the direction of rotation of the motor, thus utilizing both edges of the
cutting teeth. If the reversing switch is not fitted the motor can
be reversed by a qualified electrician removing the terminal cover
and changing over two wires in the terminal block which will be
exposed. The disposer, whilst earthed through the three-pin plug
and socket, should be earthed independently.

The Bathroom

Perhaps one of the most encouraging forward trends today in
home life is the great interest being shown by householders in the
furnishing and equipment of the bathroom. This is possibly the
result of the consistent—and persistent—policy of the manufacturers of the bathroom fitments from the bath to the tooth-
brush rack. The design and quality of their products has increased
and they have advertised widely and well. Public response has

sharpened competition and today there is a wonderful selection from which the householder can make his choice if he decides to re-model his plumbing installation.

BATHS

Enamelled Cast Iron

There is an attractive display of baths to be seen in the showrooms of most plumbers' merchants, baths to suit every purpose, taste and purse.

Most baths are manufactured in enamelled cast iron in various lengths to suit personal preference, available space or the decor of the house. They may have flat rims, rolled rims and the latest type has an almost flat bottom. This has many advantages over the conventional curved bath. First, the shallow 'step' makes it safe for the oldest and for the youngest members of the family. Then, with its flat bottom, it's safer for taking a shower. A shallow bath saves space and makes the bathroom look larger. One such type is shown in Fig. 29.

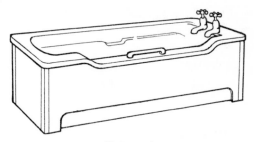

Fig. 29   Shallow bath in enamelled cast-iron

Another new bath available is a porcelain enamelled one-piece apron bath. This bath has no tap holes and is supplied with hot and cold water through a spout outlet controlled by concealed valves. It must be ordered for a left- or right-hand corner as required because it obviously cannot be turned round like the normal bath with the detachable front apron.

Pressed Steel Baths

The modern steel bath is pressed out of one piece of steel and then vitreous enamelled. There are no feet to the bath; it is cushioned into two cradles lined with felt. The bath stands quite rigidly and it will withstand all hot water temperatures. It is less costly than the cast iron bath.

BATH COLOURS

Baths are available in a range of colours as well as in white. The normal range is cream, primrose, green, blue, light coral, peony red, grey, turquoise. The price varies with the colour, i.e. light coral and grey are dearer than the others and peony red the most expensive of all.

CARE OF THE BATH

A good bath deserves good treatment before and after installation. Unfortunately, much damage can be caused before the bath is fixed. It is delivered to the site usually some time before it is installed and is left out in the weather. It is liable to damage from falling materials and rough handling. When it has been fixed by the plumber it may be scratched by other tradesmen working in the bathroom. Despite efforts by progressively minded people, it still happens that due to ignorance, stupidity and carelessness many baths are damaged. The owner of a new house will be well advised to make a close inspection of all his sanitary fittings before taking over.

CARE AFTER INSTALLATION

The householder should take notice of the following advice offered by a reputable bath manufacturer. It is in the form of 'Do's and Dont's for the Housewife':

DO run a little cold water into the bath before the hot when filling it.

DO clean it immediately after use. Hard water scum and soap rings can be removed easily with a soft brush or cloth provided it is done at once.

DO add bath salts while the bath is filling and stir to make sure they are completely dissolved.

DON'T use harsh, gritty or abrasive cleaners which may eventually damage the protective glossy surface. Should the bath have become dirty for any reason a cleaner which is specially prepared for enamelled baths is recommended.

DON'T use toilet preparation or chemicals in the bath which have an acid or strong alkaline content.

DON'T try to remove stains with lavatory cleaners which are not intended for use on baths.

BATHS MADE FROM 'PERSPEX'

Domestic baths made from 'Perspex' ICI's cast acrylic sheet, are produced by several manufacturers, and are stocked by leading builders' merchants throughout the country. Although designs and prices vary, there are some features which are common to all baths made from 'Perspex'.

Baths made from 'Perspex' are not expensive. The price of a standard white bath in 'Perspex' is comparable to that of its enamelled counterpart. Where coloured luxury baths are being considered a bath made from 'Perspex' offers a considerable saving in cost.

Because 'Perspex' is cast against plate glass, it has a superb surface finish with no ripples or blemishes. The colour goes right through the material and will not wear off. It will not stain, rust or corrode. It is unaffected by bath salts, and because it is non-porous its surface will not retain bacteria.

Light in Weight

Baths made from 'Perspex' weigh as little as 14 kg, saving handling, transport and installation costs both in private houses and multi-storey buildings. Although these baths are light in weight they are completely stable once installed. A substantial cradle is provided which supports the bath both underneath and round the rim, and the cradle is included in the price of the bath. Figure 30 illustrates how easy it is to transport a 'Perspex' bath.

Fig. 30   One man can handle a Perspex Bath

Easy to Maintain

The high gloss and good appearance of 'Perspex' can be preserved by cleaning with warm soapy water or detergent. When necessary mild scouring powder may be used, but some loss of surface lustre must be expected in time. This lustre can be renewed by polishing the surface using a liquid metal polish or a soft cloth. If a deep scratch is accidentally made, it can be rubbed out with a mild abrasive or, in an extreme case, with wire wool or emery paper, and the polished surface can be completely restored by rubbing with liquid metal polish.

Economic
Because 'Perspex' is a good thermal insulator, the hot water stays warm longer. The material is also warm to the touch.

Caution
Baths made from 'Perspex' are affected by extremes of heat, such as are generated by lighted cigarettes and burning matches, and these will cause marks on the surface. Lighted cigarettes should not therefore be placed on the surround or allowed to fall into the bath. Some dry-cleaning agents and paint strippers will damage 'Perspex'.

INSTALLATION AND PLUMBING INSTRUCTIONS
There are no special problems connected with the installation of baths made from 'Perspex', but some allowance must be made for the thermal expansion and contraction. Plumbers should pay particular attention to the fixing instructions which most manufacturers issue. In general the following points should be observed.

Installation
An unsupported bath made from 'Perspex' lacks stability because of its low weight and must therefore be securely fixed to the supporting cradle which the manufacturer provides. The bath should be levelled and secured to its cradle according to the maker's instructions. The cradle should be fixed to the floor via the supporting legs of the cradle and/or to the wall along the top rear member. All surfaces of the bath cradle which are in contact with the bath are lined with felt which should not be removed or disturbed. This felt interlayer prevents creaking which could be caused by the bath rubbing against its cradle.

Creaking can also occur when adjacent side panels rub against one another at the corners or against the underside of the bath flange. The rubbing can be avoided by slightly trimming the side panels and binding the edges with cloth tape.

When the side panels are fitted to the bath cradle (see Fig. 31), it is important to provide clearance holes through the panels for

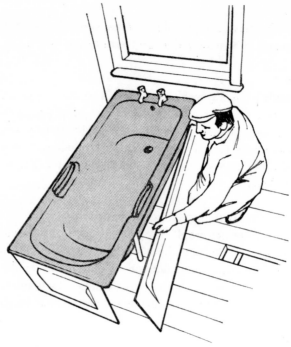

Fig.\[31   Installing a Perspex Bath

fixing to allow for thermal movement. Full support must be provided on the underside of the panels when drilling these holes.

When the bath is fitted flush with the wall, the final seal should be made using a silicone sealant. Small tubes of this material are available from most builders' merchants or ironmongers. For trade use there is a gun cartridge grade available: 'Silicone Building Sealant' which is readily available from builders' merchants. Alternatively most builders' merchants or ironmongers supply a variety of specially shaped PVC strips which can be used to make the final seal.

Tiling

The walls around a bath made from 'Perspex' can be tiled, in the normal way following the tile adhesive manufacturer's instructions. The tiles should preferably be laid so that the lower horizontal edge of the tiling lies below the rim of the bath. In this case the tiling can be undertaken prior to the installation of the bath.

If the tiling is to be carried out after the bath has been installed, the bath should be protected to prevent accidental scratching of the surface of the bath. Some tile adhesives contain solvents which can damage the surface of 'Perspex' and care should be taken to ensure that any adhesive accidentally falling into the bath is quickly removed. The effects of any slight surface damage may be removed by the use of a liquid metal polish.

Plumbing

When fitting the services to a bath made from 'Perspex' acrylic sheet care must be taken to avoid damaging the material and also to avoid fitting the services in such a way that damage to the bath could occur in service.

Waste Pipe

Normal sealing compounds can be used between the flange of the waste-pipe fitting and the bath, but it is recommended that a washer of some resilient material, such as rubber or polythene, be used between the nut on the underside and the bath itself. Moderate pressure only should be used to tighten the nut, care being taken to avoid excessive leverage which would occur if long handled pipe wrenches or spanners were used.

Where a metal trap and waste-pipe are used they must be accurately aligned to avoid imposing a twisting stress on the bath. It is essential to ensure sufficient flexibility in the plumbing to allow the trap and waste fitting to move with slight thermal movements of the bath otherwise there is a danger of cracking around the waste-pipe flange hole in service.

If a short length of iron piping is used, the system will be too rigid. This problem of providing resilience can be completely overcome by using plastics waste-pipe in conjunction with a plastics or metal waste trap. The use of suitably reinforced polythene or flexible PVC pipe for the overflow connection to the trap is recommended so that the effect of any misalignment is absorbed in its resilience rather than imposed as a stress on the bath.

Taps

For the normal types of tap no special precautions are necessary other than the provision of a resilient washer between the nut and the bath.

Some types of mixer installations and hand shower fittings are considerably bigger than normal taps and, if used as grab handles by the bath occupant, could impose sufficient leverage to the bath flange to cause damage. When fittings of this type are installed they must be secured through a reinforcing member on the underside of the bath flange.

Warning

Whenever a blow lamp is being used during the plumbing operations care must be taken to ensure that the flame is kept well away from the bath.

WASHBASINS

It was perhaps a sad reflection on the designers of sanitary ware that many of the washbasins manufactured in this country during the past 30 years presented both the housewives and the plumbers with problems. The housewife found it impossible to keep the basin properly cleaned because of awkward corners, crevices and the bad siting of the taps, while the plumber had difficulty in fixing the services and waste pipe.

However, in recent years the manufacturers have given the matter attention and sought the help of experts in design, with the result that the new washbasins are pleasant to look at as well as being functional.

Washbasins can be obtained in glazed fireclay, vitreous china, porcelain enamelled cast iron, pressed steel and stainless steel and more recently in plastics. The range of designs is extensive—as is of course the range of prices.

A type which is becoming very popular is the *vanity basin* (Fig. 32). The one illustrated has the bowl fitted flush into a plastic top having a moulded black skirting, bullnosed front edge and

Fig. 32   Vanity basin

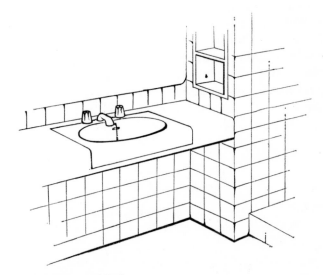

Fig. 33   A modern washbasin

shaped ends. The unit has two drawers and is supported on polished beechwood legs. Another type is a basin with a spacious table top formed from square eggshell finish tiles, with a wooden cabinet beneath.

Washbasins are being fitted in bedrooms and guest rooms today as well as in the bathroom and the pleasant modern types with splashbacks and mirrors will grace any room (Fig. 33).

It has been suggested that wherever there is a w.c. there should be a washbasin. Furthermore, it is recommended that the tap of the washbasin should be operated by a foot pedal so that the user of the w.c. can wash his or her hands before flushing the cistern. We believe that with the attractive little washbasins now available, one could be placed in every w.c. compartment, even if it was provided with but one cold water tap.

WATER CLOSETS

The modern w.c. pan is designed to be functional, unobtrusive and easy to clean. They are available in earthenware, fireclay, stainless steel and vitreous china. So far, there are no plastic w.c.s, but this might be only a matter of time.

The most commonly used type of w.c. is the washdown pedestal, so called because the flush of water washes and cleanses the whole of the internal surface of the pan. Referring to Fig. 34A, the water from the flushing cistern enters the flush pipe horn and is directed round the flushing rim and then washes down the internal surface. The water seal is, of course, the barrier which prevents drain gas from entering the house.

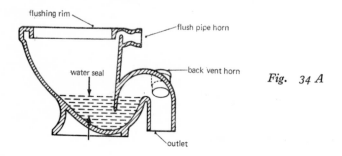

Fig.   34 A

The clanging noise of the w.c. cistern being operated and the rush of water into and out of the pan, especially at night, can be something of a nuisance. If this is a problem, it can be best overcome by the installation of a modern type siphonic w.c. pan. The seal of the trap of this type is much deeper than that of the washdown closet, thus giving a large bowl of water and a limited exposed area. A normal flush would not be sufficient to thoroughly cleanse down the fitting and leave such a large bowl re-charged with water. The contents of the pan are therefore removed by siphonic action. The action is started by the impulse of the water flush and the contents of the bowl are removed completely and silently. A typical modern siphonic w.c. is shown in Fig. 34B.

Another type of w.c. which deserves more popularity is the bracket w.c. which, as shown in Fig. 34C, is fixed on brackets clear of the wall, thus avoiding the joint between the floor and the pan. Because the pan is virtually fixed to the wall there is no chance of it cracking due to movement of the floor. The pan is of the washdown type.

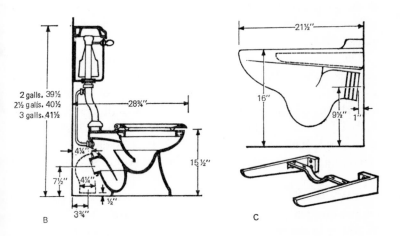

Fig. 34   A B and C   Types of w.c.s

W.C. Suite of Advanced Design

In Fig. 35 a close coupled w.c. suite is illustrated. It is the combination of a plastic cistern with a pottery washdown pedestal w.c. pan. It incorporates a silent flush of 'hydromatic' action—a design of ducts and channels which direct the water in correct volume to the right places to effect controlled maximum flushing efficiency. The washdown pan is manufactured with the trap to British Standard Specification to eliminate the risk of blockage. It is a free standing unit, only 736 mm high and projecting 710 mm from the wall. Being of low height and short projection it is easy to fit under the window in the average w.c. compartment and can be installed in many awkward places, where previously only a high level suite could be accommodated.

The suite has the smooth flowing lines and shape of contemporary design and it has the maximum hygienic qualities. Even the fixing screws are domed to avoid dust-traps and the whole suite can be easily and quickly wiped clean. Two screws at the base of the pan hold the complete suite firmly in position.

The cistern is glossy black, robust and, being plastic, is noncorroding; it bolts directly to the pan without need for brackets or flush pipe. An easy pressure on the cistern handle will immediately operate the polythene siphon mechanism to give a positive action flush.

The w.c. is fitted with an attractively shaped seat which has been designed to blend with the contemporary lines of the whole suite. It is made from what the manufacturers claim to be a virtually unbreakable material. The seat is flexible and needs no buffers. It has a light, smooth surface which is very easy to keep clean. The material from which it is made is a bad conductor of heat, therefore the seat is not as chilly as some other types.

It is a simple matter to fix the seat by means of its adjustable sliding bolt with wing nuts and washers. There are no hinge rods to be cut as the fixing bolts are adjustable in the socket.

The hinges are streamlined to make them easy to wipe clean. The seat has a cover made from strong flexible material which

Fig. 35   A close-coupled w.c. suite

completely overlaps it, thus completing the streamlined appearance of the suite.

In addition to the black plastic cistern and white ceramic pan the w.c. can also be supplied with a ceramic cistern and matching pan in white and six standard pastel shades. The seat is supplied only in black, but the seat cover is available in black, deep red, deep blue, white, ivory, green, primrose, pink and turquoise.

Toilet Aids to the Aged and Infirm
Manufacturers of plumbing appliances are always ready to co-operate in producing gadgets and aids to help the aged and infirm. Three such aids are illustrated in Fig. 36.

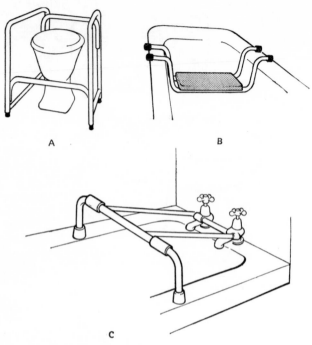

Fig. 36   Toilet aids for the infirm
A   The 'Seataid'
B   Bath safety seat
C   Bath safety rail

THE BIDET

This is a sanitary fitting designed on lines similar to a pedestal
w.c. pan, but is intended primarily as an ablution fitment for use
by women in matters of personal hygiene. It is used in a great
many homes and hotels on the Continent, but is beginning to find
favour in this country among the middle and upper class groups.
It should only be used for ablutionary purposes and therefore
may be connected to a waste pipe and not a soil pipe.

Figure 37 shows a modern type of bidet. It is provided with a
douche jet in an upward direction for ablution, and this is controlled by hot and cold valves. The bidet does not have a seat and

Fig. 37   The bidet

warm water can be used to flush the fitment so that the rim is rendered comfortable to the person sitting on it.

Important: The bidet must be installed in such a way as to prevent contamination of water supply. The recommended method of connecting a bidet is laid down in Section 328 (b) of the British Standard Code of Practice CP 310 : 1965, which reads as follows:

Appliances with submergable inlets
'Baths, wash basins, sinks and similar appliances which have not the ½″ air gap between spillover level and level of discharge of the taps, mentioned in Sub-Clause 327b, and appliances with submergable inlets, such as sluicing sinks and bed pan washers as used in hospitals laboratory sinks and bidets should be supplied with hot water and cold water by a method which involves no danger of contamination by back flow or back-siphonage. The cold water should be supplied from a storage cistern through a separate pipe which supplies only the appliance in question or a number of similar appliances at the same level or from a flushing cistern. The hot water should be supplied from a hot water storage cistern or cylinder by a separate pipe which supplies only the appliance or a number of similar appliances at the same level, and where a cylinder is used the pipe should be connected directly into it at a point which is higher than the appliance. Appliances are deemed to be at the same level if their water inlets are at the same level and if their spillover levels are the same, so that a range of identical bidets on the same flow level could be supplied by the same pipes, *but a bidet in a bathroom should not be supplied by the pipes supplying the bath or wash basin.*'

9 | The Shower Bath in the Home

There is no doubt that the shower has become one of the foremost trends in bathroom equipment in Britain today. It is indispensable in the U.S. and in the Commonwealth and many overseas countries British bathrooms have hitherto lagged behind in this respect, but the almost universal use of showers in H.M. Forces and in industry —viz. pithead baths, foundries and other 'dirty' industries—has brought its advantages to the notice of a large section of the population. Also, because of the widespread use of showers in hotels, holiday camps, sports grounds and schools and colleges, a generation is growing up that will probably insist on showers in its homes.

The lack of interest in showers which once existed in this country was due to unawareness of the pleasure, health and convenience that they afford, and of their efficiency and economy. It must be admitted however, that the simple precautions necessary to ensure their successful use have not been sufficiently publicized.

The shower today is not a luxury; it is the commonsense, hygienic method of bathing. It is not expensive to install, and the saving on fuel bills which it makes possible is by no means the least of its attractions.

It may therefore be appropriate to set down the advantages of the shower, particularly for those householders who will not be content to wait too long for it to come into the home. Plumbers will do well to encourage this new trend for it could bring a substantial increase in business. Apart from the fact that in itself the shower improves the facilities of the normal bathroom the shower can be installed in homes where, for reasons of space and convenience, the usual type of bath cannot be provided.

The salient advantages of the shower, not necessarily in order of importance, are:

1. It is hygienic and pleasant to use.
2. The shower is much cheaper to operate as water consumption is considerably less than with the traditional bath. This is particularly important with regard to hot water, and where water softeners are installed.
3. It follows that more baths may be obtained in succession without an increase in the heating or storage capacity.
4. The shower takes less time to use, thus alleviating bathroom queues.
5. It occupies considerably less space than a bath.
6. Because it is simple to adjust the water temperature of the shower, the possibility of a person catching cold after a hot bath is very remote, particularly if the shower is turned to cool before finishing.

First Essentials

For a shower bath the hot and cold water must be mixed to give a constant supply at a selected temperature, and it is most essential that a means of varying this temperature between fully hot and fully cold should be provided. This can be done by using a mixing valve which equalizes the pressures of the hot and cold water. An obvious way of doing this with the ordinary domestic system is to arrange that the cold water supply to the mixing fitting be taken from the same cold cistern that feeds the hot water system. It must be understood that Bye-laws prohibit the mixing of cold water direct from the main with hot water from a gravity system.

It is also essential that there is an adequate 'head', or pressure, of water at the shower itself, and this is determined by the height of the cold water cistern above the shower outlet. Generally, it can be taken that if the bottom of the cold water cistern is a minimum 2·5 m above the floor of the bathroom, a satisfactory shower can be obtained. If a greater height than this is possible, so much the better. If the cold water side of the mixing fitting is fed from a single pipe from the supply cistern, it will avoid the possibility of other draw-off points, causing a drop in pressure and a consequent sudden increase in temperature at the shower.

MIXING FITTINGS

These are divided broadly into two classes (1) the mixer, which consists of a pair of orthodox hot and cold screw-down taps with their outlets joined together by means of a 'breeching' or mixing chamber, and (2) the mixing valve, which combines the two taps or valves in one, is operated by a single control handle, and allows any temperature between hot and cold to be selected manually by moving a pointer round a scale marked 'cold', 'tepid' and 'hot'.

With the mixer fitting no visual indication of the temperature is given, and this, allied to the fact that two valves have to be adjusted, makes it slower and very much less convenient and positive than the mixing valve.

Mixing valves are divided into two classes, the manual or non-thermostatic, and the thermostatic, the latter being provided with a thermostat, the purpose of which is to compensate automatically for changes in the temperature of the incoming hot and cold supplies. It is necessary with this type of valve to provide a stop tap in the outlet for the purpose of shutting off the shower which in turn, often requires the provision of non-return valves in the inlets to prevent 'backing' of hot water up the cold water pipe, due to gravity circulation or convection.

The manually operated non-thermostatic mixing valve is an orthodox screw-down-type valve operated by a threaded spindle. It has an indicator marked 'shut', 'cold', 'tepid' and 'hot' and should preferably open in an anti-clockwise direction as in an ordinary household water tap (see Fig. 38). This valve possesses the twofold advantage of not only permitting a choice of any variation of temperature between hot and cold, but also shutting off both supplies simultaneously, all by the use of a single handle. British Standard 1415 stipulates that it must be turned through cold before tepid or hot can be reached and lays down a minimum performance and capacity. Purchasers are recommended to insist upon compliance with this standard. A good quality mixing valve

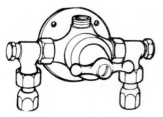

Fig. 38 Manually operated mixing valve

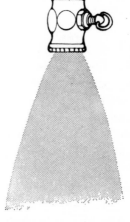

Fig. 39 Shower sprayer

of this type has renewable control valve washers and should prefer-ably have renewable seatings. Moreover, it will not need an outlet stop tap or inlet check valves, or strainers. It may incorporate in the inlet connections built-in means of shutting off the incoming supplies whilst the valve is being dismantled for servicing.

The Bye-law, which requires equal pressures on hot and cold supplies, will remove the prejudice that has existed in some minds against mixing valves of the manual type. Proper sizing and layout of pipes and connections will reduce to negligible proportions any fluctuation of temperature due to variations in flow.

There are many new and attractive mixing valves on the market including one in plastics. The householder can shop around to suit his own fancy and pocket. It can be said that all those valves, expensive and inexpensive, manufactured by well-known firms and marketed by established plumbers' merchants are reliable and safe.

SHOWER ROSE OR SHOWER SPRAY

The part of the shower fitting from which the water finally issues may be referred to as the shower head and is available in two types. There is the 'rose' type, often referred to as the 'watering' can type. This can take different forms but in each the water comes out in jets from a large number of small holes. The ad-vantages of the rose are that it will operate at a somewhat lower head of water and, if large enough, can give an extremely heavy shower; it is often slightly cheaper in cost than the sprayer.

The other type of shower head is the 'sprayer' graphically illustrated in Fig. 39, which by utilizing centrifugal force forms a spray of what might be likened to raindrops. The sprayer makes use of a small number of comparatively large holes. Much more economical in the use of water, its consumption is predetermined. Its centrifugal action has the effect of assisting the mixing of hot and cold water, and its small consumption will damp down sudden variations of temperature that may be caused by 'heavy-handed' manipulation of the mixing valve handle. The spray of aerated drops is extremely pleasant and invigorating. The most popular type passes 7 litres per minute, of which only half is hot and half cold. The sprayer is much less liable to choke up, can easily be cleaned out and is almost indestructible in use. It usually has a cap end that can be changed to vary the volume and size of spray.

THE SHOWER IN CONJUNCTION WITH THE BATH

Practically any type of shower can be used over a bath. For the sake of convenience and safety, the type of bath which has a fairly wide and flat bottom is to be preferred. It is also an advantage if the bath is fixed in a corner or in an alcove, and is of the type which has a flat rim, or roll, over which the walls will project slightly, thus ensuring that water cannot run between the bath and the walls.

In order to prevent water from the shower spraying or splashing over the front of the bath on to the floor, some type of shield is required. This may take the form of a glass panel which can be hinged to swing outwards, or, as is more usual and considerably cheaper, a curtain rail and waterproof curtain can be used. The curtain will need to be long enough to fall inside the bath, and wide enough to cover the whole length of the bath. If the bath is fitted in an alcove, a straight rail of tube with a flange at each end will be required. If the bath is fitted in a corner, the rail will need to be semi-rectangular, and the 'return' end, across the bath, will be secured to the back wall. In this case the curtain must be wide enough to draw across both the front and the return end.

In the case of a bath which stands clear of the walls, a curtain rail of fully rectangular shape can be provided. Curtain rails of circular form are obtainable, but although they permit a person to stand under the shower, they allow insufficient space for soaping and rinsing.

It is usual to fix the shower at the end above the bath taps and to take the water supplies to it from the service pipes feeding the latter. Both mixer fittings and mixing valves are made in 22 mm size, and arranged for the double purpose of filling the bath and feeding the shower, as required. It is more common, however, to provide a separate 15 mm mixing valve for the shower and a pair of 22 mm taps, or a 22 mm mixer fitting, for the bath.

Whatever the arrangement may be, it must be remembered that, so long as mixing takes place and the hot water comes from a low pressure storage system, the cold water connection must not be made direct to the main.

THE SHOWER BATH AS A COMPLETE UNIT

Where the shower is to take the place of, or is to be separate from, the slipper bath, a shower cubicle can be built in as an annexe to the bathroom (see Fig. 40), or in any other suitable place in the house. The essentials here are a receiving tray at floor level, which can be obtained in fireclay, enamelled iron, stainless steel or fibreglass. The tray may also be of tiled construction or built from timber and lined with a suitable material. A 42 mm waste and trap and an overflow connection will be required. Three walls can be tiled or rendered waterproof by other suitable means, and the fourth, or front, side can be provided with a waterproof curtain sufficiently long to fall inside the receiving tray. Curtains are now available in plastics, in a large range of attractive colours and patterns. Shower enclosures can also be built of glass panels with metal framework.

The shower fitting itself can either be of the 'overhead' or 'shoulder height' type, the latter allowing a person to take a

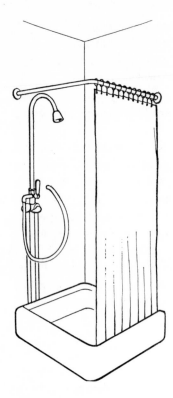

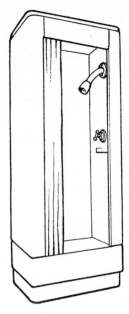

Fig. 40   Built-in shower cubicle

Fig. 41   Prefabricated shower cabinet

shower without necessarily wetting the head. Fittings are also available with both overhead and shoulder height sprays, either or both of which can be selected by means of a control lever.

Completely prefabricated shower cabinets with plinth, receiving tray, front curtains, mixing valve and shower head are available. These can be set anywhere in the house—even on a bedroom carpet—and only require connecting up to hot and cold supplies and waste pipe. No building work of any kind is required. They can be purchased in dismantled sections, allowing them to be taken upstairs and through narrow doorways, to where they can easily and quickly be assembled. It is preferable that cabinets of this type be provided with a top to them, as this helps to confine the vapour that rises from a shower. It is also important that they should be rustproof. For this reason the use of aluminium is of great advantage for it cannot rust and is very light to handle. This type of cabinet is illustrated in Fig. 41.

The absence of a domestic hot water supply system does not rule out a shower. Showers can be operated from certain types of gas and electric water heaters, and can then utilize pressure direct from the cold water main. Mixing arrangements are available for such showers, and, as both hot and cold come direct from the main, regulations are not contravened.

One maker of self-contained shower cabinets supplies them complete with either gas or electric water heater, and a tapping is often taken from the same heater to supply hot water to a nearby washbasin.

Children almost invariably love showers, but in the case of very young infants it is advisable to have the waste of the receiving tray fitted with a tubular 'standing' overflow which will allow the water to build up to the level of the top of this tube before overflowing. This makes a very satisfactory bath for infants. One make of aluminium shower cabinet on the market is fitted with this type of standing overflow which permits a depth of approximately four inches of water to build up in the receiving tray.

LOCATION OF SHOWERS IN THE HOUSE

The shower need not necessarily be confined to upper floors. The ground floor has many advantages, not the least of which is that it almost invariably ensures an adequate head of water.

An unused cloakroom or pantry is often ideal, and many houses without bathrooms have had a shower fitted in an opening off the kitchen or in a corner of the kitchen itself, where the absence of any of the usual forms of space heating is quite unnoticed. For many elderly persons who find getting in and out of a slippery bath hazardous, a shower is ideal; particularly so when sited on a ground floor.

Installing a Shower

A shower can be installed in a space as small as 760 mm square. In fact, this often makes it worth while installing a shower as an extra washing facility.

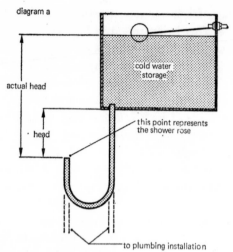

Fig. 42 '*Head*' *or pressure of water*

THE 'HEAD' OR PRESSURE OF WATER

If a 'U' tube is fed from the underside of a water cistern (Fig. 42) and the open end of the 'U' tube is at the same level as the level of the tank, no water will flow. If a metre is cut from the open end of the 'U' tube then the water will flow and a small fountain of water will spray from the end of the 'U' tube. If we now cut 3 m from the open end of the 'U' tube it can be appreciated that water will try to reach its own level and create a much higher fountain.

The amount that is cut from the tube is known as the 'head' or pressure. In the first instance we would have had a one-metre head and in the second instance a three-metre head, and the greater the head the faster the flow and the more water available.

INSTALLATION

No shower fitting can work satisfactorily unless the installation is right. Careful attention to the following simple requirements is needed only once, and will ensure many years of trouble-free service.

Measure the Head

Make sure that there is sufficient head or pressure available. You must position the shower rose at a minimum distance of 1 m between the base of the cold water cistern (Fig. 43). (You can ignore the position of the hot water cylinder on the hot supply; it is its source, as cold water, that matters.) This is the absolute minimum figure and will probably only be acceptable where pipe runs are short and a gentle wetting shower is acceptable.

Normally the figure should be 1·5 m or more which should provide a spray of 4·5–6·5 litres per minute. However, where even the figure of 1 m is impossible to achieve a booster can be installed.

Where the gravity flow is insufficient, a shower booster is the answer. The booster lifts the available water from the mixer to the shower rose, resulting in a reasonable flow of water instead of a mere trickle. The function performed by the shower booster does not pressurize the flow, which would require some three times the volume of water that is normally available in British domestic installations. It is important that the booster is not starved of water and the minimum flow of blended water at the mixer outlet should not be less than 6 litres per minute. The pressure, however, may be as low as that provided by a 200 mm head when measured from the cold water level in the shower cistern to the rose (Fig. 44).

The good shower booster should be fully automatic and go into operation when either the hot or cold tap is turned on.

It must be safe and all working parts protected inside the wall-mounted casing. Only a low voltage cable should enter the bathroom and the fused transformer mounted above the ceiling or in an adjacent room.

A shower booster is easily installed and the Barking Brassware 'Flomatic' is regarded as being suitable in every way. Fix the sealed unit to the wall as shown and connect up the transformer. Quick installation and correct operation are only assured when installed as shown in the diagram.

The 'Flomatic' Shower Booster can be used with Bath and Shower Mixer Fittings and Shower Controllers.

Fig. 43　Recommended 'Head'

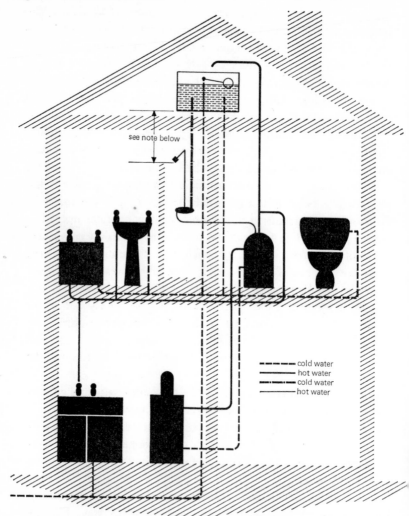

see note below

cold water
hot water
cold water
hot water

Note:　1.5 m is the recommended height from the underside of the cistern to the shower rose. If the pipe runs are short this may be reduced to a minimum of 1 m.

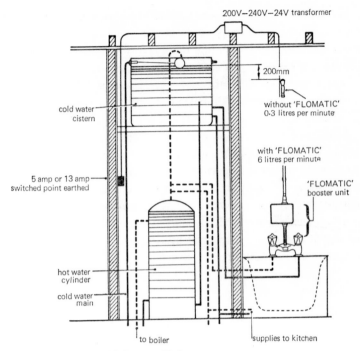

200V–240V–24V transformer

200mm

without 'FLOMATIC'
0·3 litres per minute

with 'FLOMATIC'
6 litres per minute

'FLOMATIC'
booster unit

cold water
cistern

5 amp or 13 amp
switched point earthed

hot water
cylinder

cold water
main

to boiler

supplies to kitchen

Fig. 44   The 'Flomatic' Booster Unit

Equal Pressures

Hot and cold water supply pressures to the Shower Controller
need to be about equal. If, as is most likely, the hot water system
is fed from a storage cistern, then the cold water supply to the
Controller **must** come from the same cistern, or from one along-
side it. It is technically wrong and dangerous, and contrary to the
Bye-laws of water authorities, to connect the hot water side of the
Controller to the cistern and the cold water side to the mains
supply.

Get the Flows Right

Eliminate long lengths of pipes in which static hot water rapidly
cools and that infuriating wait while tepid water issues from the
shower rose.

You should also note that the connections with existing pipe runs which feed other taps or draw-offs could lead to intermittent water starvation and so to fluctuations in the shower temperature. Ideally it is better to run independent hot and cold water supplies to the Controller from the hot water storage cylinder and the cold water cistern. The elements of a satisfactory household system are shown, with the pipe runs to the shower.

All Controllers are fitted with a maximum temperature limiting device which will enable you to set the maximum temperature of the spray to suit your particular requirements. Hot water boilers can be set at different temperatures for various purposes and this will affect the shower temperature. The maximum temperature limiting device is an essential safety feature when boilers installed for the dual purpose of central heating and water supply are set at maximum temperature.

10 | Soil and Waste Pipe Systems

The owner of a house should know something about the system used to dispose of waste water and human excrement from his home. His personal comfort and that of his family is dependent to a great extent on the efficient working of this disposal system. It matters very little to him what happens to the waste matter after it has passed from the plumbing system of his home, although he would in fact probably find it a surprisingly fascinating subject.

The house is a small self-contained unit, one of many thousands connected by a drainage system to the town sewer. This chapter is concerned only with the system within the house.

DEFINITIONS
A waste pipe takes the discharge from bath, washbasin, kitchen sink, bidet, washing machine and dishwashing machine.
A soil pipe takes the discharge from the w.c. pan.

As with water supply, there are specific Bye-laws which regulate the installation of soil and waste pipes.

EXCLUSION OF FOUL AIR
Despite the fact that present-day medical evidence discounts the once predominant opinion that drain gas can give rise to epidemics and is detrimental to health, there is no person who would want foul air to penetrate his home. The smell of drains is obnoxious and it is imperative that it should be sealed off at all the appliances used for excremental, ablutionary and domestic purposes. Protection against drain gas infiltration is attained by that simple appliance called a trap. A trap is formed by a depression or a U-bend which will retain water in the trap but not interfere with the flow of water through the pipes. Traps may be separate fittings or

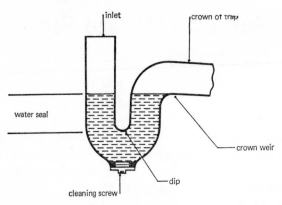

Fig. 45   Details of a P trap

embodied in the appliance itself. In Fig. 45 a P trap is illustrated. The important part of the trap is the water seal, which forms the barrier against the passage of drain air through the trap. While that seal is maintained all will be well but if the water level is depressed below the point marked 'dip' on the illustration, then drain gas can infiltrate into the house. Traps are fixed to kitchen sinks, washbasins and baths and are an integral part of the w.c. pan and the bidet.

LOSS OF WATER SEAL OF A TRAP
The loss of the vital water seal of a trap may be due to one or more of the following reasons:
1.   Self-siphonage
2.   Induced siphonage
3.   Evaporation
   The chief problems are to avoid self-siphonage, by which individual appliances suck out their own seals when they discharge, and induced siphonage by which the discharge of one fitting 'pulls' out the seal of another fitting.
   In long spells of hot, dry weather the evaporation of a trap may occur if a house is left unoccupied for any length of time. The only remedy is to arrange for someone to flush the appliances from time to time.

The Development of Sanitation

Sanitary installations in the existing homes in the UK are of a wide variety and may be classified as bad, sub-standard, satisfactory, reasonably good and good. Much depended on the standard of the houses in which the plumbing was installed. In the old days, the property developers had to produce low-cost houses in order to sell them. There was severe competition and this pulled down standards. Houses were sold cheaply and much of the interior work was shoddy. This applied to plumbing both in design and workmanship. The bath and basin wastes discharged into open 'hopper heads' just beneath the bathroom window. The hopper also took the discharge of rainwater from the roof gutters. The waste pipes were fixed to the external wall, very often insecurely causing them to droop between the fixings. The hopper became fouled and gave off smells in the summer. In the winter the whole system would freeze-up.

Government regulations and normal development have brought about considerable improvement both in design of systems and the manufacture of materials, fittings and appliances used in plumbing. The advent of plastics in particular has improved plumbing, making light work of its installation, and widening the range of fittings, thereby reducing the labour time involved.

Plastics are used almost exclusively for soil and waste installations in new homes today and although there is still the test of time to be considered, most of the early problems in its use have been overcome and it seems certain that it will be the material of the future in the whole field of plumbing.

SINGLE-STACK PLUMBING

The system of sanitary plumbing being installed in most new houses is known as 'Single Stack' so called because all the fitments of the house discharge into a single pipe and no vent pipes are connected to the individual appliances. The purpose of the system is to reduce the complexity and cost of plumbing.

The efficiency of single-stack plumbing depends on the close grouping of the fitments and keeping the length of branch pipes to a minimum. Careful attention to design and installation procedure is essential and the basic requirements must be observed.

The Building Research Station has produced a Digest (No. 80) setting out its recommendations on single-stack plumbing and these should form the basis for any such installation.

The design curve shown in Fig. 46 gives the gradients of waste pipes from washbasins. The risk of self-siphonage from washbasins is much more closely dependent on the design of the branch connection to the stack than it is for other appliances. The diameter of the bore of the pipe, and its length and fall are all important factors. Waste pipes from washbasins being of relatively small diameter (30 mm) run fully charged and by doing so cause suction at the trap end of the discharge. This can be remedied by limiting the length and slope of the pipe. Figure 46 gives maximum allowable slopes for varying lengths of nominal 30 mm waste pipe used in conjunction with a 75 mm seal P-trap.

If the basin is more than 1·68 m from the stack suction at the

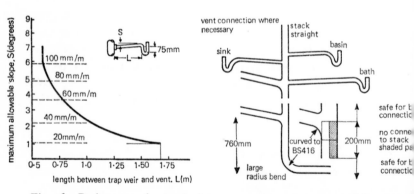

Fig. 46   Design curve for nominal 30 mm wastes and 75 mm seal P-traps connected to single BS lavatory basins. The minimum desirable slope is 20 mm. (the slopes recommended are allowable maxima but the pipes need not be fixed at exactly the gradients read off the graph.)

Fig. 47   Design of single-stack system—main features

trap can be reduced if a short tail piece of 30 mm pipe discharges into a 40 mm or 50 mm pipe connected to the stack. This will prevent the pipe running full.

Self-sealing traps are available and these avoid the complete self-siphonage of the discharge by permitting some of the waste water to drain back to reform the trap seal.

S-traps and small radius bends in the waste pipe should be avoided wherever possible as they tend to increase self-siphonage.

Water closet branches do not run full so no matter what length they are there is no danger of self-siphonage. Nevertheless, the shape of the w.c. branch connection can induce siphonage action on branches to other appliances in the stack. The w.c. connection should be swept in the direction of the flow (see Fig. 47).

DIGEST 80 RECOMMENDATIONS

The Building Research Station recommendations include:

1. Waste pipes longer than the recommended maximum length of 1·68 m should be vented, or a larger diameter waste pipe or suitable resealing trap should be used. Any bends should be not less than 75 mm radius to the centre line.

2. Bath and sink wastes should have 40 mm nominal traps and waste pipes and the trap seal should be 75 mm. Self-siphonage problems should not arise so the length and slope of the waste branch is not vital, but sediment might accumulate in long pipes so access for cleansing should be provided.

3. The w.c. connections should be swept in the direction of the flow. Fittings should have a minimum sweep of at least 5 mm radius. W.C. branches up to 6 m long have been used successfully.

4. The bend at the foot of the stack should be of large radius. The minimum recommended radius for 100 mm stack pipes is 200 mm. The vertical distance between the lowest branch connection and invert of drain to be at least 760 mm.

5. To avoid back pressure there should be no offsets in stacks below the topmost appliances unless venting is provided to relieve any back pressure. Offsets above the topmost appliance are of no significance.

Comprehensive Designing Based on Practical Research

The Marley Plumbing team who carried out practical experiments and developed their findings into practical designs and fittings, have given valuable advice to plumbers through the media of lectures and publications.

THE COLLAR BOSS

One intriguing development in single-stack plumbing is the Marley Collar Boss. This soil pipe fitting has been designed to overcome a number of different installation problems which occur now that the Building Regulations require all soil pipes in new construction to be located inside buildings.

The BRS Digest 80 recommends that small diameter branch wastes with orifices of connections exposed to the w.c. discharge do not join the soil pipe in the 200 mm area below the centre of the w.c. branch (see Fig. 47). This often means that the bath waste pipework has to offset through the floor and enter the stack via a boss branch fitted below or in the ceiling space.

Apart from increasing the labour content of the plumbing installation a bath waste passing down through the floor can create structural difficulties for other building trades.

The collar boss has an annular cavity in the main body which receives water from the branch wastes and this deflected down and around the sloping shoulders into the vertical stack. Air always present in the annular chamber removes any tendency for self-siphonage to occur while the effluent is flowing from the branch waste and the normal rate of discharge from the sanitary fitment is unaffected. Discharge from the w.c. is prevented from making contact with the annular space or boss connections by the wall of the internal socket. Details of the collar boss are given in Fig. 48A.

INSTALLATION OF THE COLLAR BOSS

When the collar boss has to be fitted high up under the throat of a 100 mm branch the spigot of the branch may be solvent welded to the lower internal socket (Fig. 48B).

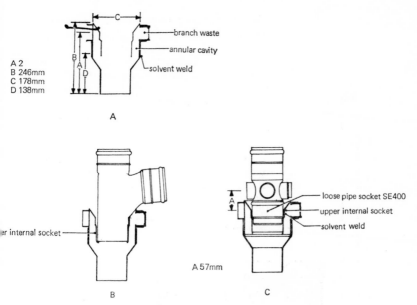

Fig. 48   The Marley Collar boss

Adjustment to the position of the collar boss may be achieved by solvent welding an offcut of the length required from a loose pipe socket into the upper internal socket in order to provide a ring seal joint (Fig. 48c).

This technique may also be adapted to enable the collar boss to be used in conjunction with any of the 100 mm boss branch fittings in the soil pipe range to close up the centre to centre dimensions of the bosses occurring on the same side of the stack or in any other position through 360 degrees (Fig. 48c). Moulded boss upstands not in use may be cut off where necessary.

In Fig. 49 a typical house installation is shown. Detailed diagrams and catalogue describing the fittings may be obtained from Marley Plumbing, Dickley Lane, Lenham, Kent.

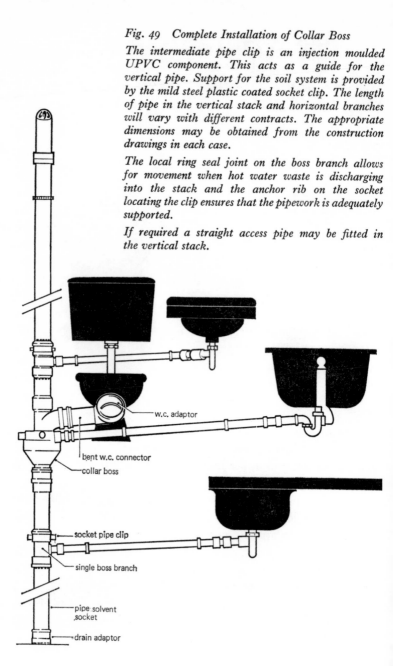

Fig. 49   Complete Installation of Collar Boss

The intermediate pipe clip is an injection moulded UPVC component. This acts as a guide for the vertical pipe. Support for the soil system is provided by the mild steel plastic coated socket clip. The length of pipe in the vertical stack and horizontal branches will vary with different contracts. The appropriate dimensions may be obtained from the construction drawings in each case.

The local ring seal joint on the boss branch allows for movement when hot water waste is discharging into the stack and the anchor rib on the socket locating the clip ensures that the pipework is adequately supported.

If required a straight access pipe may be fitted in the vertical stack.

w.c. adaptor

bent w.c. connector

collar boss

socket pipe clip

single boss branch

pipe solvent socket

drain adaptor

11 | Rainwater Disposal

In years gone by the house-builder had little regard for rainwater pipes or gutters. They were necessary however, and the main thing was to get them fixed as cheaply as possible—after all, you could hardly sell a house on its rainwater pipes and gutters! Even on better class, architect designed properties, very little thought was given to the position, size or design of rainwater pipes and gutters. Many a house having an exhilarating or even exciting elevation has been mutilated by a festoon of pipes and gutters.

Cheap materials, bad sizing and inferior fixing of rainwater gutters and pipes has caused damage to property. Leaking joints, pipes and metal gutters fixed without painting and in a position that painting the back of them has been impossible has caused them to rust away after a relatively short period of time.

NEED FOR CARE IN FIXING

The purpose of a rainwater gutter is to catch all the rain falling on a roof during the heavier downfall and to convey it to the outlets, where it empties into the down pipe, which in turn should be capable of conducting all the water to the drain, without any spilling out of the joints and soaking the brickwork.

All joints must be made properly and if the pipes and gutters are of metal they must be painted. They should be fixed in such a manner that it is possible to clean them and repaint them at regular intervals. Gutters must have an adequate fall to take the water to the outlets and to make them self-cleaning. It is essential that the outlets of the gutters should be protected with wire balloons to prevent leaves and other matter from choking the downpipe.

PLASTICS RAINWATER GOODS

Possibly the most progressive move forward has been the design and supply of plastics rainwater goods, which provide many advantages over those made from other materials.

By using plastics materials it has been possible to employ greatly improved design techniques resulting in a considerably improved appearance and substantial savings in erection costs. Guttering is simply snapped into a bracket which has a moulded-in clip joint and a butyl rubber strip provides a 100 per cent watertight seal. In this way the need for gutter bolts has been removed.

Plastics have eliminated corrosion problems—a constant worry with cast iron. Hence there is no need for surface protection and for this reason the guttering and downpiping can be self-coloured.

A comprehensive guide to rainwater gutter and downpipe installation follows. It is intended for the installer and the householder, explaining step by step the procedure and techniques. For simplicity we have restricted the instructions to one type only manufactured by Marley Plumbing Ltd.

The most serious losses occasioned by a failure of conventional guttering and downpiping are due not only to corrosion but to accidents through storage and transportation, and breakage during fitting. The percentage of breakages with plastics rainwater goods is negligible, and their lightness in weight makes transportation and erection on site a simple and trouble-free job.

Gutter Installation

The Marley gutter joint with separate jointing strap located between notches on spigot and socket is shown in Fig. 50. The strap compresses the spigot down against the synthetic rubber seal which is secured in every socket before the products leave the factory. When correctly assembled the joint cannot pull apart, and it will absorb the expansion and contraction of the gutter while maintaining a watertight seal.

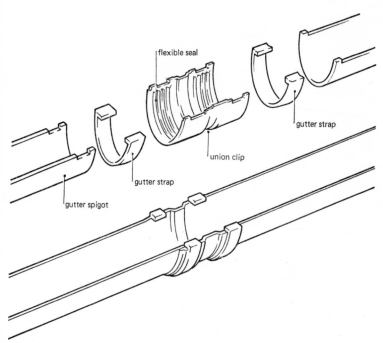

Fig. 50

POSITION OF THE UNDERGROUND DRAIN

The location of the underground drain is an important factor in setting out a gutter installation. The trapped gulley or drain socket at ground level automatically determines the centre line of the gutter outlet which is normally immediately above. This is shown in Fig. 51.

POSITION OF RAINWATER PIPES

Considerations affecting the position of rainwater pipes are:
1. Architectural requirements
2. Maximum flow capacity of the gutter
3. Underground drainage design
4. The accuracy in which the timber fascia is fixed to the rafters

Item 4 is particularly important yet often overlooked. Fascia boards that are not level cause a large gap to develop between the gutter and the eaves course of tiles (see Fig. 52). This occurs

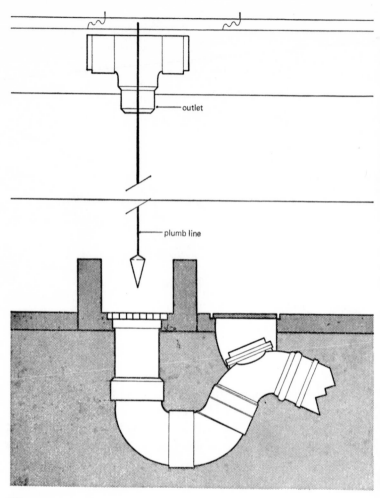

Fig. 51

when the plumber is fitting to gradients which are opposed to the slope of the fascia.

FIXING THE BRACKETS TO A TIMBER FASCIA
Plumbers occasionally fix the brackets and install the gutter before the roof is tiled. There is a risk of damage to uPVC gutters during the roof tiling operation as well as a great accumulation of debris

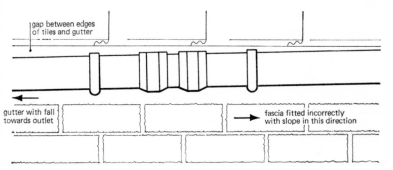

gap between edges
of tiles and gutter

gutter with fall
towards outlet

fascia fitted incorrectly
with slope in this direction

Fig. 52

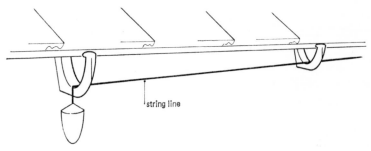

string line

Fig. 53

collecting in the gutter. It is advised that the sequence of events
be arranged that the roof is tiled and the final painting of the fascia
board completed before the plumber fixes the brackets and installs
the gutter while the scaffolding is still in position. A good plumber
can be relied upon not to damage the finished paintwork while
fixing the gutter. The brackets may be fixed in the usual way with
a string line acting as a guide to alignment for brackets between
the extreme end of the installation and the outlet of the gutter
(Fig. 53).

When fitting brackets to a fall, the end bracket at the high point
should be secured as close as possible to the underside of the
roofing felt and projecting eaves course of tiles. The intermediate
brackets are then screwed to the fascia with zinc plated or sheradized round head screws at a maximum of 1 m centres (Fig. 54).

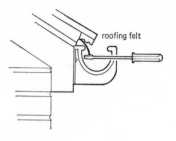

Fig. 54

POSITION OF GUTTER BRACKETS

Gutter is supplied in 3 m lengths and on long straight runs the arrangement of brackets should be as indicated in Fig. 55. The gutter union has a centre portion to accommodate the fascia bracket and this feature in combination with the 3 m double spigot lengths of gutter, provides the method of arranging the support brackets. Careful attention to detail is necessary because the union bracket has to be accurately located taking into account the small tolerance on every gutter length.

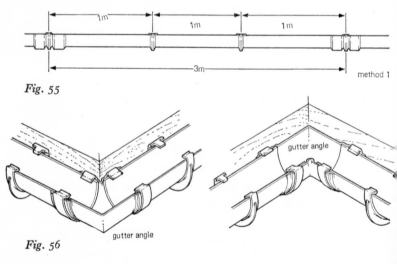

Fig. 55

Fig. 56

ANGLE

External and internal angles should have close supporting brackets on each side of the joints as shown in Fig. 56.

OUTLETS

Gutter outlets should also have brackets fitted on each side of the joints to the gutter (Fig. 57). The stopend outlet is designed to suit the fascia bracket and this type should always be installed so that the rainwater pipe may be correctly engaged with the nozzle of the outlet.

FITTING AND JOINTING THE GUTTER

Lengths of gutter are introduced into the brackets as illustrated in Fig. 58 and clipped into place under the projection at the front of the fascia brackets. As the gutter is installed the rear edge should turn into the brackets under the roofing felt in order that the gap between gutter and tiles is weathered. This prevents the rainwater from being blown against the fascia as it runs from the tiles into the gutter.

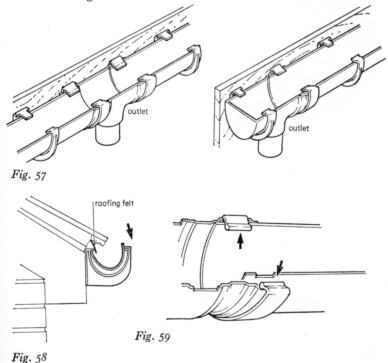

Fig. 57

Fig. 58

Fig. 59

To assemble a joint, clip the gutter strap around the socket of a fitting between the notches. Turn the spigot end of the gutter into the socket, under the back edge of the strap, so that the retaining projection fits into the notch (see Fig. 59). Ease the front edge of the gutter spigot down until it snaps under the strap. This now compresses the gutter against the pre-fixed synthetic rubber seal to form a watertight joint.

Finally line up the notches on the spigot and socket so that the strap is in the centre (Fig. 60).

CUTTING AND NOTCHING THE GUTTER

Occasionally it will be necessary to cut a length of gutter. A fine tooth saw should be used for this purpose taking care to cut straight at 90 degrees to the axis of the gutter (Fig. 61). The notches must then be cut or filed into the edges of the spigot end. A tool is available from the Marley Company for cutting notches but they can be done quite easily using a file. The dimensions of the notch are given in Fig. 62.

The notches must always be formed before attempting to complete a joint.

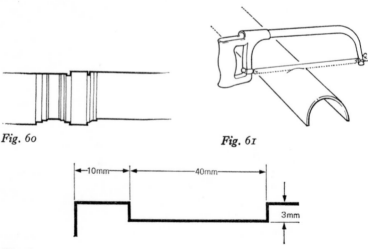

Fig. 60

Fig. 61

Fig. 62

Circular Pipe Installation

CONNECTION TO THE GUTTER OUTLET

When the gutter outlet is positioned directly above the drain, the offset must be of the correct projection passing straight back under the soffit to engage with the rainwater pipe. Ideally a ring seal should be located in the socket recess of the offset to secure and seal the connection of the two fittings (Fig. 63).

SOLVENT WELDED OFFSETS

An offset may be fabricated on site from an offset socket, offset spigot and an offcut of pipe. The procedure is as follows:

1.   Cut pipe to length and remove all rough edges (Fig. 64A)

2.   Internal surfaces of solvent weld sockets and outside of pipe ends should be wiped perfectly clean with a dry cloth

3.   Assemble the offset dry and draw pencil lines along the pipe and fittings (Fig. 64B) to ensure correct alignment

4.   Remove pipe from fittings. Apply solvent cement evenly around the spigots and inside sockets from the tube (Fig. 64C)

5.   Press pipe and fittings quickly and firmly together taking care to line up with pencil guide lines

6.   Leave the offset for several minutes before fitting into position in order that the joints may set properly

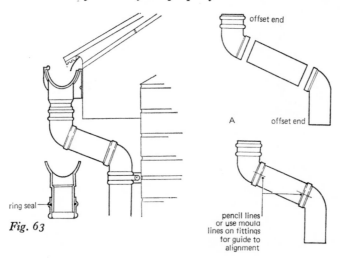

ring seal

Fig. 63

offset end

A   offset end

pencil lines
or use mould
lines on fittings
for guide to
alignment

Fig. 64 A and B   B

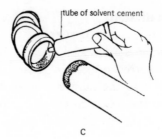

Fig. 64 C   C

CONNECTION OF OFFSET TO RAINWATER PIPE

The offset spigot is 112 mm long. This allows the socket of the offset to be pushed fully on to the nozzle of the outlet, while providing some facility for adjusting the first pipe clip. The clip is fastened around the socket, then the offset and first length of pipe are placed in position (Fig. 65).

If the holes in the pipe bracket backplate fail to come in line with a mortar joint, *do not* lower the offset on the nozzle of the outlet. Instead, measure the amount of spigot to be cut off, in order that the pipe clip may be fixed in the next joint up.

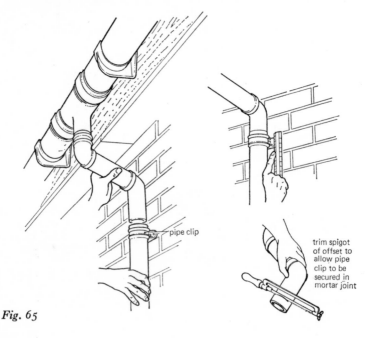

Fig. 65

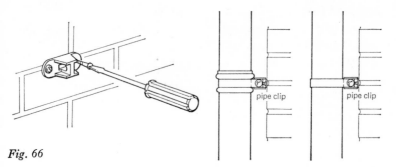

Fig. 66

LOCATION OF RAINWATER PIPE CLIPS

Pipe clips are provided to fit both the rainwater pipe, and the pipe socket.

The vertical centres of pipe clips are usually marked on the wall with the aid of a plumb line suspended from the top pipe clip position.

Pipe clip backplates, or in the case of the one piece fitting, the clip itself, are secured to the structure with two 38 or 32 mm × 10 gauge zinc plated or sheradized round-head steel screws. Purpose made fibre or plastics plugs should be inserted into the fixing holes when they have been drilled. The use of handmade soft wood plugs should be avoided Fig. 66).

The pipe clips are supplied with nuts and bolts to fasten the uPVC ring to the backplate. Every rainwater pipe should have a clip located at the socket to support the pipework system. Intermediate pipe clips should then be provided in the centre of each pipe length where it exceeds 2 m.

An expansion gap of 10 mm should be left between the end of each pipe and the bottom of the socket Fig. 67).

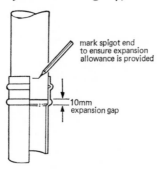

Fig. 67

CONNECTION TO THE UNDERGROUND DRAIN

Depending on the design of the system of buried drainage, rain-water pipes may terminate as follows:

1. With a shoe above the grating of a trapped gulley;
2. Jointed to the back or side inlet of a gulley trap;
3. Connected direct to the drain with an adaptor.

The connections are shown in fig. 68.

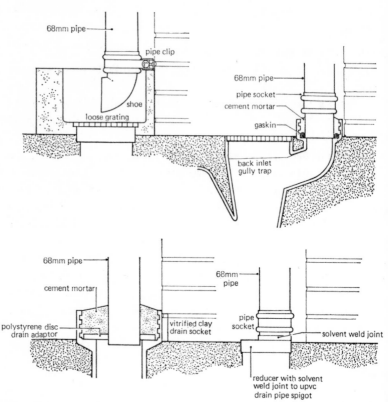

Fig. 68   Connection to the underground drain

12 | Plastics Plumbing

Plastics, although with a history of over a hundred years, is a comparatively new material in the plumbing world. Because of its lower cost in both material and labour it has moved in rather rapidly, with the result that information relating to these materials has not been digested quickly enough.

Another danger that has arisen is that various types of plastics can be used for the same application, but require different techniques for installation and jointing, just as do copper and stainless steel. Therefore, it is essential for the plumber to recognize these new plastics materials.

The plastics range of material today is vast, but for practical purposes only, the materials that are used for plumbing products are our real concern. The main emphasis must be on the plastics that make up the pipe and fittings of the installation and not so much the plastics materials of the appliance to which the system has to be connected. The reason being that individual items under the categories of storage and flushing cisterns, taps, basins and baths, generally have their own specific fixing instructions attached.

FIVE GROUPS OF PLASTICS

The plastics that are used in the manufacture of pipes and fittings for above and below ground drainage and services, can be placed into five basic groups.

1. Polyvinyl chloride (uPVC and CPVC)
2. Styrene based (ABS)
3. Polyolefin (polyethylene and polypropylene)
4. Glass reinforced plastics
5. Nylon

Group 1 is used for rainwater, soil, waste, overflow below ground drainage, cold water services and pressure pipe installations. Has a hard, smooth finish with a specific gravity of approximately 1·4.

Group 2 is used for waste runs generally of 35 mm, 42 mm and 54 mm nominal bore diameters, overflow pipes and water services. Is being used in the US for soil installations, but not in the UK. Similar appearance and feel to the plastics in Group 1, but with a specific gravity of approximately 1·1.

Group 3 is used for waste runs including laboratory work, overflow, water services and internal rainwater systems. Has a 'waxy' feel about it, and a specific gravity of 0·9 to 0·96.

Group 4 is used for rainwater roof outlets, valley type gutters and special fittings for large diameter pipe work. Can be recognized by the glass fibre reinforcements embedded in the material. Its specific gravity is 1–2 or more, depending on the glass content.

Group 5 is used sometimes for 'minibore' central heating tube and pressure pipe work. Has a similar feel and appearance to the polyolefins and a specific gravity of approximately 1·1.

IDENTIFICATION OF PLASTICS

It will be observed that out of these five groups, only the polyolefins (Group 3) has a specific gravity of less than 1·0. Hence by placing a fitting, or small offcut from the pipe in fresh water, only the items made from material in this group will float. It is essential that no air is trapped in the components when carrying out this procedure.

Both the components from Groups 1 and 2 will not float, but they can be distinguished apart by offering small shavings of the materials to a flame. The polyvinyl chloride in Group 1 will be self-extinguishing when taken away from the flame, while the styrene based material in Group 2 will continue to burn.

As already mentioned the glass reinforced plastics in Group 4 can be identified by the glass fibres embedded in the material, but as a further test press a hot metal point on its surface. Resin glass material will only char slightly whereas the effects on Groups 1, 2, 3 and 5 will be similar, only in a lesser degree, to a hot metal point pressed on to sealing wax.

The nylon plastics can be distinguished from Group 3 because they will sink in water and not burn so readily. The vapour smell when burnt is akin to burning hair!

Identification of all these plastics components by their colour is not possible, because depending on the pigments used in manufacture, a variety of colours can be produced.

It is important to be able to identify these plastics materials that are used for pipe and fittings, for each group has certain individual characteristics. For instance, chemical resistance, temperature limitation, weathering ability and coefficient of expansion, present each group with a different specification, which must be taken into consideration. Identification is also important to ensure that the correct method of jointing is applied.

In practice it has been proved that all joints of recognized design which incorporate a seal ring are suitable for making an air- or water-tight joint with all plastics piping. But the method of making a joint by using a solvent to fuse the materials together is limited to specific plastics.

The polyolefins and nylon plastics cannot be solvent welded, whereas the styrene based and polyvinyl chloride materials can. Different formulations of solvent cements are supplied for the two latter groups and should be used in accordance with the manufacturers' instructions.

With the exception of the comment on nylon, we have refrained from identifying the materials by burning and smelling the vapour, for it is felt that some experience in this field is required to ascertain positive results. Also any foreign matter in the burnt plastics could mislead one's sense of smell.

In constant association with these materials the plumber will quickly be able to recognize the polyolefins and resin glass easily by the appearance, feel and the manner in which the saw cuts them. Distinguishing between the styrene based and polyvinyl chloride is a little more difficult and very often the experienced person has to apply a basic identification test to confirm the result.

Once the identification of the plastics materials is established the recognized methods of working can be applied.

ALLOWANCE FOR EXPANSION

If expansion is not allowed for in rigid plastics pipe work, there could be a high percentage of failure in the installation, but the degree of failure could depend upon the use to which the system is put.

For instance, if the ambient and flow temperature of the pipe varies by only say 10°C, it would be debatable whether the installation would suffer any damage, even if the length of the rigid pipe run was 1·5 or 2 m.

In practice it is very seldom that these conditions can be guaranteed for the life of the installation. Therefore, maximum temperature conditions relating to the purpose of the system should always be assured.

When a rapid and a reasonable amount of expansion is taking place, the cause is generally due to very hot fluid flowing through the pipe. In these conditions plastics pipe would be more vulnerable to deformation, and unless adequate allowance is made for expansion, the pipe is likely to buckle. It could also damage or disturb the fittings locating the pipe.

Changes in surrounding temperatures also create thermal movement, especially with outside pipe and gutter installations.

Plastics Plumbing Installation

Manufacturers of plastics pipe and fittings systems issue their own fixing instructions and it is always advisable to conform to their recommendations. The allowances for thermal movement have been established, not only by theoretical calculations, but by sound practical testing.

A question that concerns many is that if an installation could be constantly moving throughout its life, surely this would be detrimental to the system? The answer is simply that if the system has been fitted to give adequate allowance for freedom of movement then under its normal working conditions for which it was designed no strain will be taking place, and the material will not be subjected to fatigue.

Obviously there will also be expansion and contraction movement in the width of the pipe work. But as this is so slight it can be disregarded for practical purposes.

With plastics piping there is a considerable temperature difference between the discharge and the outside wall of the pipe. A clear example of this is illustrated in the British Standards discharge cycling test for uPVC soil pipes. This shows that when 35 litres of water at 91°C are discharged into a 3·17 mm thick uPVC soil stack from a waste entry, over a period of 90 seconds, the hottest point of the outside pipe wall will be in the region of 70°C. Because the material has low heat transmission, the expansion of the pipe is not so great as one would expect in relation to the high temperature of the discharge. It is for this reason that plastics systems will withstand intermittent discharges of higher temperatures than the melting point of the material.

It will be seen from the foregoing that the main concern about thermal movement in plastics is related to rigid materials, which are being widely used for above surface drainage.

SOIL AND WASTE PIPES

We are going to deal only with soil, waste and drain pipes because it is in this area of plumbing that most progress has been made in the use of plastics. The tried and tested material used is unplasticized polyvinyl chloride which we will now refer to as uPVC. These pipes have been widely used in the UK for some years now and they are accepted by almost every local authority. Changes and improvements in design of components and materials are constantly taking place and the wise plumber will keep abreast with these changes by maintaining regular communication with manufacturers and trade bodies through technical literature and meetings. He should also concern himself with British Standard Code of Practice for the material and the Digests published by the Building Research Station. For comprehensive information of a practical nature he can obtain publications from the Institute of Plumbing: Scottish Mutual House, North Street, Hornchurch, Essex.

Types of Systems

The uPVC systems for soil pipes are classified by their methods of jointing and are placed in two groups: (1) Joint ring and (2) Solvent weld. The joint ring systems may include fittings in the range where a solvent weld is required and similarly solvent weld will require expansion joints in the forms of joint ring sockets to allow for thermal movement. A typical joint ring system is illustrated in Fig. 69. There are a few other types all of which are effective and suitable.

JOINT RING SYSTEMS

The joint ring illustrated fits in the annular space of the pipe socket. When the other pipe is inserted in the socket, a coupling nut locks the ring on the socket and spigot surfaces, forming a gas and watertight seal.

It is important to know that the design of ring seals differs from one to another manufacturer and they are seldom interchangeable. It is essential that the correct ring be used and that the manufacturer's instructions be carefully followed. Even when the joint rings are despatched from the manufacturer already fitted into the sockets, the plumber should carefully check to see that the ring is correctly engaged and undamaged before he makes the joint.

When the ring is supplied separately it should be cleaned before

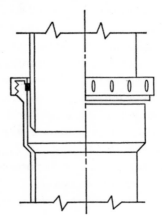

Fig. 69

being inserted in the recess in the socket both of which of course should also be cleaned.

Joint Assembly
There is a very wide range of soil and waste pipe fittings available in the plastics industry and most manufacturers can provide the plumber with lavish brochures showing their complete range and giving detailed dimensions and fixing instructions.

One general point which must never be overlooked in assembling plastics pipes and fittings is the maker's instructions giving the depth to which the spigot should be inserted in the socket. These instructions are in some cases given on an adhesive tape attached to the spigot of the fitting. In other cases the depth is indicated by a mark on the spigot end.

In all installations the spigot end of a pipe secured by a joint ring should always be directed in the same line as the flow of water from the appliance.

Spigot ends must be chamfered to permit easy assembly. Moulded fittings have their spigot ends already chamfered but the plumber must prepare pipe ends himself.

Plastics pipes can be cut with a hacksaw or better still, a fine toothed saw. With the latter it is less difficult to make the absolutely square cut so important in correct assembly of pipes and fittings.

When the pipe has been cut a pencil guide line should be made around the pipe about 7 mm from the end. Then with a fine rasp or a coarse file a chamfer can be formed working from the guide line to the end of the pipe, avoiding making a sharp edge.

The pipe must be inserted in the fitting to the correct depth and this can be achieved by marking with a pencil the depth recommended by the manufacturer or alternatively, the pipe may be inserted to the full depth, marked with the pencil and then withdrawn 10 mm. A bold line is then drawn round the pipe at the top of the socket (see Fig. 70). This method provides a better guide line for preparing the pipe for assembly with the socket.

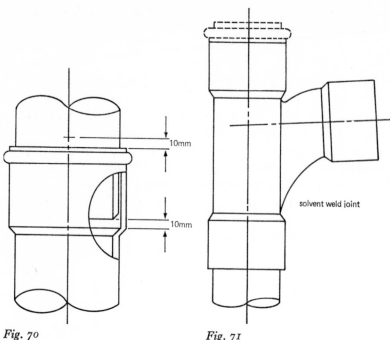

Fig. 70   *Fig. 71*

Making the Joint

The chamfer on the spigot is lubricated generously with petroleum jelly, soft soap or silicone grease and with the clean joint ring in place in the cleaned socket, the spigot is lined up with the socket. With a slight twisting motion the spigot is pushed firmly past the joint ring and into the socket until the insertion depth mark is level with the face of the socket.

Coupling Nut Compression Type Joint Seal

The compression type of joint is made by a locknut which is slipped on to the spigot end after which the joint ring is also put on the pipe end. The spigot is then entered in the socket to the prescribed depth and the joint completed by pushing the rubber ring into the socket and tightening the locknut. The manufacturers of this type of joint issue explicit instructions which must be followed in all assembly work.

SOLVENT WELD SYSTEM

The solvent weld system is satisfactory providing that due allowance is made for thermal movement in the installation. This is
achieved by the use of expansion joints of the ring seal type at
strategic points.

In a solvent weld joint the spigot should fit very closely with
the socket. In some cases it will be found that when pushed together
dry the spigot will only enter the socket to about half its depth but
when the solvent is applied its effect will allow penetration of the
spigot to full depth.

With the solvent weld system it is permissible to make a joint
against the direction of the flow in vertical and horizontal pipework installations (see Fig. 71). There are all-socketed fittings and
fittings with spigot ends to which the pipes are attached by using
loose sockets. When properly made the joint is homogeneous and
rigid with the spigot butted against the internal shoulder of the
socket leaving a smooth full and uninterrupted pipe bore.

Care must be taken to make a solvent weld correctly and the
procedure is as follows:

1.   Remove any dust and swarf from the pipe end and the socket
both of which should be cleaned thoroughly. The manufacturers
of plastics supply a special cleaning fluid which acts as a degreasing
agent and removes the glossy surface from uPVC in readiness for
the solvent welding operation.

2.   If a pipe has to be cut the end should be square and even
and all rough edges smoothed before applying solvent.

3.   Apply one coat of uPVC solvent cement to the external surface
of the spigot and the internal surface of the socket.

4.   Push the spigot into the socket with a slight twisting movement
until it reaches the full depth of the socket.

5.   Wipe off any surplus solvent cement immediately.

With careful treatment it should be possible to handle the joint
in two or three minutes. If possible however, the system should
be left to stand for 24 hours before being put into operation.

Some manufacturers recommend the application of two coats
of solvent cement.

13 | Copper Tubes

The resistance of copper to corrosion is due to the formation by natural processes of a protective film which in nearly all cases renders the metal safe from attack by the atmosphere and from any water, gas or soil with which it may be in contact. The film is primarily an oxidized layer which forms a protective skin on both the outside and inside of copper tubes and ensures not only a long life for the pipe, but also that it will not contaminate drinking water or require any additional treatment for protection when installed in contact with the usual building materials or normal types of soil.

Copper tubes cannot rust and do not require painting, which saves cost and, in the case of hot water pipes, avoids the unpleasant smell of warm paint. In certain cases where the pipes are run on the surface the attractive appearance of the metal can be exploited to fit in with the surrounding decorative features. The trend in modern plumbing is to conceal pipes as much as possible, with the result that they are installed in chases or are buried in walls and floors. Concrete, lime and lime plasters and cement mortar have no harmful effect on copper but there are certain acid soils and materials which are known to be corrosive to all metals.

In addition to their corrosion-resisting properties, copper tubes possess a combination of physical characteristics. The ductility of the metal enables them to be manipulated with ease, while the strength of even light gauge tubes ensures that they will withstand pressures far higher than those to be found in normal pipe services. They will withstand considerable internal and external pressures and adjust themselves to irregularities and settlements in soils or buildings without risk of fractures occurring.

In certain cases, tubes are subjected to expansion and contraction due to changes in temperature, and restraint of the consequent movement at various points in the installation may set up stresses in the pipes. Copper combines sufficient strength and elasticity to prevent any permanent deformation such as that which occurs in tubes of softer metals under similar conditions. In the case of heating installations carried out in copper tubes, there is economy in the amount of metal used, with a consequent saving in cost, weight and space; a smaller mass of metal to be heated, less radiation surface for heat loss, thereby effecting a saving in fuel. The ease by which the tubes can be handled, manipulated and jointed means lower labour costs and reduction in the number of fittings required.

The very smooth surface of a solid drawn copper tube is an important feature particularly in a water pipe, because of the low frictional resistance it offers to the flow of the water, and in waste pipes because it reduces the risk of blockages to a minimum. In hard water districts the calcium carbonate deposits do not adhere so quickly or firmly to the smooth interior surface of a copper tube and therefore the removal of scale that might form is a simple matter.

From a decorative point of view, the smooth non-rusting exterior surface has much to commend it and it can be polished easily and it readily takes a plated finish. The small diameter tubes and fittings give a neat and unobtrusive appearance.

A point of some importance arising from the smooth bore of a copper is that it affords in conjunction with the strength and ductility of copper, a measure of protection against frost bursting. It is of course not claimed by the manufacturers of copper tubes that they will not burst under extreme conditions. A good plumber would never expose any tube installation to extreme conditions.

An important development came with the manufacture of long-length copper tubes in 'dead soft' temper. These tubes are supplied in coils of 20 m.

Jointing Copper Tubes

The present widespread use of copper for all forms of pipework in plumbing is a result of the development of suitable means of jointing light gauge tubes. The joints commonly used today in house plumbing are manipulative and non-manipulative compression fittings and capillary joints.

British Standard 864, Part 2: 1971 'Capillary Fittings and Compression Fittings of Copper and Copper Alloy, for Use with Light Gauge Copper Tube' gives the general dimensions and classifies them as non-manipulative compression fittings Type A, manipulative compression fittings Type B, and capillary soldered fittings, and states that the fittings shall be of copper or a suitable corrosion resisting alloy. A Table sets out the allowable hydraulic working pressures and temperatures for these forms of joints, but it may be of interest that many of the fittings, both capillary and compression, can be used at higher temperatures and pressures. Under such conditions, however, the manufacturers should be consulted regarding any special requirements necessary to ensure their products giving satisfactory service.

In the past some confusion has arisen over the method of stating the sizes of tees or crosses. To overcome this a standard method has now been adopted by all manufacturers as follows:

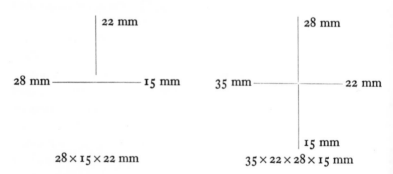

A good type of joint should not in any way restrict the bore of the tube and in addition should preferably be so made as to allow easy dismantling for maintenance or other purposes.

COMPRESSION JOINTS

The non-manipulative compression joint, as the name implies, does not require any working of the tube end other than cutting it square. The joint is made tight by means of a loose ring or sleeve which grips the outside wall of the tube when the coupling nut is tightened.

In the manipulative type of compression joint the end of the tube is flared, cupped or belled with special forming tools and is compressed by means of a coupling nut against the shaped end of corresponding section on the fitting or a loose thimble.

Figure 72 shows typical joints of the non-manipulative type. A joint of this type is made by slipping the coupling nut and compression ring on to the squared end of the tube and inserting it into the mouth of the fitting up to the internal shoulder. The

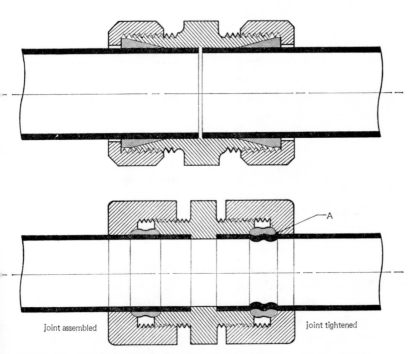

joint assembled   joint tightened

Fig. 72 Non-manipulative compression joints

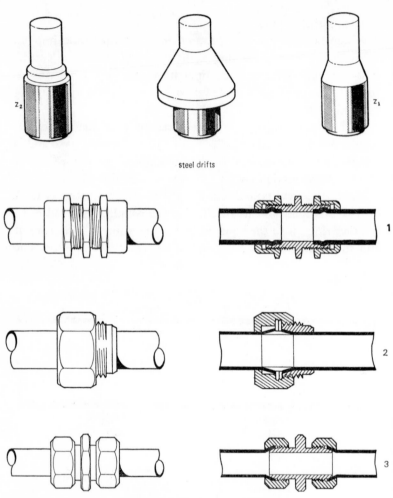

steel drifts

Fig. 73   *Manipulative compression joints*

coupling nut is then screwed up tight with a spanner, causing the edge, or edges, of the compression ring to bite into the copper tube. The effect (A) is shown in exaggerated form.

In Fig. 73 are shown three main types of manipulative compression joints. Joint No. 1 is prepared by cutting the tube to length, squaring off the end and after slipping the coupling nut on, a special expanding tool is inserted into the tube. A tommy-bar in the tool is then turned in its housing to the stop; by this action the steel balls in the tool are forced outwards and at the same time are rotated, thereby swaging a bead in the tube wall. The tool is removed from the tube by bringing the tommy-bar back to its original position. The tube is then inserted in the mouth of the fitting and the joint completed by screwing up the coupling nut.

In joint No. 2, the centre ferrule is machined from copper, bronze or brass and the angle or degree of taper matches that formed on the tube end after it has been expanded by the steel drift. The mouth of the male portion of the fitting and the friction ring inside the coupling nut are similarly machined, so that the jointing faces all marry up. The union is assembled by screwing up the coupling nut with a spanner, the body of the fitting being held at the same time with another spanner.

In preparing joint No. 3, the coupling nut is first slipped over the tube end, a split collar die is placed on the tube and secured by tightening up the side nuts; the tube end is then opened by the drift Z and after withdrawing this, the second drift Z is used to form the belled or cupped mouth as shown. The collar is removed by unbolting and the tube end pulled up tight to the body by screwing up the coupling nut, thus making a mechanically sound joint.

CAPILLARY SOLDERED JOINTS
Since the soldered or sweated joints—or as they should be called—capillary joints were introduced in this country, development has been taken up on a considerable scale and now the joint has come to be generally accepted as neat, sound and economical. Capillary fittings are suitable for hot and cold water services and waste pipes. They are made from copper and copper alloys.

Capillary fittings are constructed upon the basic principle of capillary attraction, which provides the means by which molten solder is drawn into the narrow space between the two closely fitting metal surfaces of the exterior of the tube ends and the interior of the jointing piece. The joint can be made either in the horizontal or the vertical position. The closeness of the fit is the main factor in ensuring capillary attraction, and it is therefore of the greatest importance that the fittings are those intended for the exact gauges and diameters of the tubes being used.

The certainty of an exact fit is provided for by the British Standard for Light Gauge Copper Tubes (BS 2871 : Part 1 and BS 864 : Part 2) which specifies both wall thicknesses and external diameters and states the permissible tolerances; and is still further assured by BS 864, Part 2 : 1971 'Capillary Fittings and Compression Fittings for Use with Light Gauge Copper Tubes', which similarly specifies the dimensions of fittings.

It was thought at one time that there might be a likelihood of corrosion due to electrolytic action taking place between the copper of the tubes or fittings and the jointing solder. This fear was unfounded however, for it is most unlikely that any appreciable action could take place with normal waters and a properly made joint, since the amount of solder left exposed to the action of the water inside the pipe, or to condensation on the outside, is so small as to be negligible. If the water is likely to be of such a corrosive nature that there is a danger of electrolytic action, it may be assumed that it is sufficiently corrosive to act upon plain metal and should therefore be submitted to preliminary examination no matter what type of joint is used.

Years of experience have now proved that capillary joints are perfectly satisfactory for hot water and heating installations. Where especially long pipe runs are encountered in such installations, provision should be made to take up the movement due to temperature variations, by means of expansion bends or expansion joints. These are hardly ever likely to be required for installations in the ordinary dwelling house.

ASSEMBLING CAPILLARY JOINTS

The assembly of any type of capillary joint consists, briefly, of cutting square the tube ends, thoroughly cleaning them and the inside of the fitting, fluxing, inserting the tubes in the fitting and heating with a blow lamp. When heat is applied, solder is fed

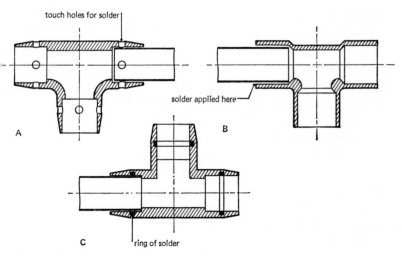

Fig. 74   Capillary joints for copper tubes

into the joint from solder wire applied (A) at a touch hole in the fitting, (B) at the mouth of the fitting, or (C) from a reservoir of solder already within the fitting. These fittings are illustrated in Fig. 74. As an alternative to feeding solder in by these means, the joint can be made with solder paint, applied evenly to the tube after cleaning and prior to inserting in the fitting.

Much emphasis is placed on the need for close attention to every detail in making capillary joints even although it appears to be a very simple process. The steps are as follows:

1.   The tube must be cut square to sit evenly on the shoulder at the bottom of the socket, and all rough edges formed by the sawing operation should be removed by file or reamer. For sawing, a special vice is obtainable which has interchangeable jaws to hold tubes of all sizes. The vice holds any length of tube, and because the saw blade moves between close guides, there is less burr to be removed and no trueing up is required after the cut is made.

2.   The exterior surface of the tube at its ends, and the interior surface of the fitting must be scoured to remove all traces of dirt and oxide, which would prevent the solder from adhering to the

metal. This operation should be carried out with steel wool or sandpaper but emery paper or emery cloth should not be used.

3.   The metal surfaces to be united on both tube and fitting are next evenly coated with flux to prevent the surfaces from oxidizing when heat is applied. It is most important that the flux used should be one approved by the fittings manufacturer.

4.   The tube ends are then inserted in the fitting and it is important that their ends bed squarely on the socket shoulders.

5.   Heat is applied by playing the flame of a blowlamp upon the outside of the socket until it has reached an even temperature all round to melt the solder easily. The temperature may be determined when applying the solder externally (Figs. A and B), by watching for flux vapours. When these appear it is time to apply the solder at the touch hole (type A) or at the mouth of the socket (type B). The socket should not be overheated, as overheating could break down the flux, oxidize the cleaned surfaces and burn the solder. In type A, if the solder does not run freely into the touch hole and does not appear at the mouth of the socket, or if in type B does not disappear freely into the socket before it finally floods up to the mouth, the joint should be regarded with suspicion and it would be advisable to re-make it.

When using type C it is only necessary to apply heat after having completed carefully the cleaning and fluxing operations. The joint should be closely inspected to check that the solder has crept out to the mouth of the socket, forming a complete and even ring of solder there.

Bending Copper Tubes

One of the advantages in the use of copper tubes for building services is the ease with which they can be bent either by bending machine or spring, and in the case of larger diameter tubes, by means of sand filling, resin filling, low melting point filler alloys or mandrel bending machines.

For a proper understanding of what is involved in bending, the reader should clearly understand what deformations take place when a copper tube is bent. The walls of a straight tube are parallel and must remain parallel after bending if the true round section of the tube is to be maintained in the bend. The original length of the tube o–o remains unaltered after bending only along the centre line of the tube. It follows that the inside, or throat, of the bend is shortened and compressed and the outside, or back, is lengthened and stretched (see Fig. 75). From this it will be

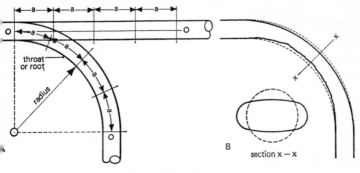

eory of bending

True and deformed bends
A True bend.Each division a represents a 'throw' in making the bend.
B Deformation of bend in unsupported tubes.

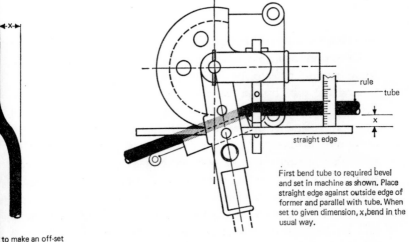

to make an off-set

First bend tube to required bevel and set in machine as shown. Place straight edge against outside edge of former and parallel with tube. When set to given dimension, x, bend in the usual way.

Fig. 75   Bending techniques

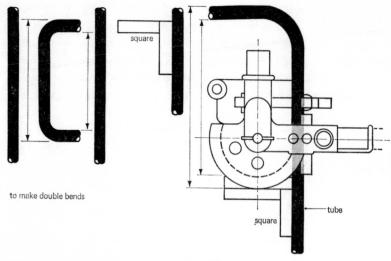

to make double bends

square

tube

square

To bend to inside measurement, y, mark tube as shown. Place square on mark and insert in bending machine so that the square touches the inside of the groove of the former. Bend as usual.

To bend to outside measurement, z, mark the tube as shown. Place square on mark and insert in bending machine so that the square touches the outside edge of the former. Bend as usual.

Fig 75   Bending techniques

seen that the tube will collapse in the bend unless precautions are taken to prevent it. Therefore, it is necessary to support the tube while bending takes place. This support is provided by filling or loading the tube by the material just mentioned or the use of a bending machine, of which there are many on the market, will prove an economic proposition, particularly for sizes of tube up to 54 mm diameter. These machines work by hand power or through a ratchet action or gear and employ special formers and back guides to ensure that the tube, when pulled to the necessary angle, maintains its true diameter and shape throughout the length of the bend. It is important that in using any machine, the formers and guides should be maintained in good condition and well lubricated. This also applies to bending springs.

Fitting Copper Tubes

Advantages of light gauge copper tubes are the ease with which they can be installed and their neat appearance. These points can be appreciated where numerous tubes run parallel on walls or ceilings. They should always be accurately lined up, be parallel and plumb and kept equidistant if at all possible. The use of purpose-made fittings and bends makes this an easy matter. Where pipes change direction through 90 degrees, or are off-set to pass some break or obstruction in the building, it is generally better to use bends rather than sharp elbows.

Where several pipes are running together, they should be left far enough apart to allow sufficient clearance for the securing of fixing clips.

In setting out bends or off-sets, it is always worthwhile making a full sized drawing, on the bench or floor, to which the bending points on the straight pipes can be set to obtain the correct angles easily and quickly.

One additional advantage of using light gauge copper tubes is the ease with which off-site prefabrication can be done. This means a considerable saving in labour as such units can be assembled in jigs, easily transported to the site, and call for a minimum of site labour for fixing.

Copper and brass fixing clips for use with light gauge copper tubes are made in a variety of patterns.

The coefficient of thermal expansion of copper is $16.6 \times 10^{-6}/°C$, that is to say a length increase of approximately 3.5 mm for every 3 m run of tube for a temperature rise of $50°C$. While this amount is slightly greater than that of iron, it is considerably less than that of lead or plastic tubing. In the general run of heating and hot water installations, the many bends and off-sets which occur, accommodate the amount of thermal movement that will take place due to temperature variations.

Occasional complaints of noise transmission arise as a result of high water pressures, faulty ball valves or other terminal points or where pumps or boosters are installed. The trouble can be overcome by using flexible connectors, called vibration eliminators, at terminal ends and on pump inlets and outlets. In some cases, however, noise transmission may occur as a result of inadequate use of fixing or spacing clips. Taking the Imperial measurements given in the British Standard Code of Practice CP 310 : 1965 and converting these into metric terms, the fixing spaces for light gauge copper tubes are as follows:

Diameter mm	Horizontal run m	Vertical run m
12	1·2	1·5
15	1·2	1·5
18	1·2	1·5
22	2·0	2·5
28	2·0	2·5
35	2·5	3·0

Where these dimensions are adhered to, noise transmission will not occur under normal service conditions.

14 | Screwed Pipes and Fittings

THE BYE-LAWS
First it is necessary to know that the Bye-laws require that the pipes used shall conform to certain standards of quality. The relevant Bye-law for mild steel or wrought iron pipes is as follows:

'Every distributing pipe of wrought iron or steel not in contact with the soil shall comply with requirements for pipes of water (medium) quality contained in British Standard 788, 1938, for wrought iron tubes and tubulars or the requirements for Class B pipes contained in British Standard 1387, 1947, for steel tubes and tubulars and every such distributing pipe in contact with the soil shall comply with the requirements contained in the said British Standards for pipes of steam (heavy) quality and for Class C pipes respectively.'

For fittings the Bye-law states:

'Every malleable cast iron fitting used in connection with any pipe to which the preceding paragraphs of this Bye-law relate, shall comply with the relevant requirements of British Standard 1256/143, 1969, for malleable cast iron fittings and cast copper alloy pipe fittings.

Every wrought fitting of iron or steel used in connection with any pipe shall comply with British Standard 1740, 1951, for wrought pipe fittings and shall be of heavy weight when used in connection with steam (heavy) quality or Class C pipes.'

PROTECTION

Unprotected iron and steel pipes are liable to severe corrosion by some waters and internal incrustation may in time be formed which will entirely close the bore of small diameter pipes. Discoloration of the water might also occur with certain waters. All pipes should be galvanized, and where they are in contact with the soil be also coated with bitumen and wrapped with a spiral wrapping of glass tissue impregnated with bitumen. Pipes should never be fixed in contact with magnesium oxychloride flooring or with Keene's cement.

PIPE THREADS

The screw threads on pipes are referred to as gas threads, and the manufacturers make them to the requirements of British Standard Specification No. 21.

The screw threads on the pipes or, for that matter, all external threads are termed 'male' while the internal screw threads of pipe fittings are referred to as 'female'. It is important to use these terms when ordering fittings for any kind of plumbing work.

PIPE FITTINGS

A very wide range of pipe fittings is available and they are manufactured in wrought iron and in malleable cast iron.

Wrought-iron fittings are products of a special process from which semi-molten metal, mixed with slag, is passed through squeezers and rolled to the desired section, from which the fittings are produced.

Malleable cast-iron fittings are cast from white iron and subsequently annealed. This is a heat-treatment process which gives the fitting a certain elasticity. Such fittings are easily recognized by the strengthening bead round the edge of the fitting. They are of pleasing appearance and because they are cheaper than wrought-iron fittings they are widely used in the plumbing trade.

In Fig. 76 the range of pipe fittings available is illustrated. Those with the beads are malleable fittings. The letter M refers to male and the letter F to female. This is the method of description employed by the trade as stated earlier.

RULES FOR READING

It is important to know how to 'read' sizes of tee-pieces, crosses and side outlet fittings, etc.

Tee-pieces: When one size is specified it applies to each outlet, i.e. an equal tee is illustrated at A in Fig. 76.

When two sizes are specified, the first applies to both ends of the barrel and the second to the branch (see B).

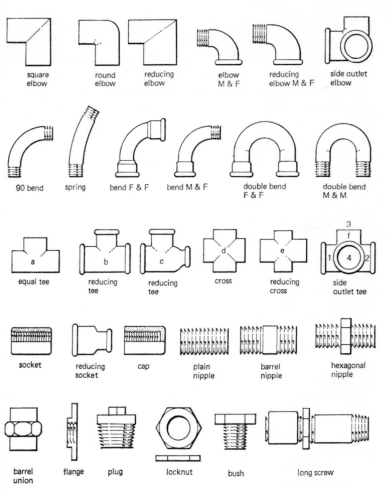

Fig. 76 Pipe fittings

When three sizes are specified the first two apply to the ends
of the barrel, the larger end being specified first.

Crosses: When one size is specified it applies to all the ends of
the cross.

When two sizes are specified the first applies to one pair of
opposite ends, the second to the other pair, the larger pair being

specified first. When four sizes are specified the first two apply to one pair of opposite ends and the second two to the other pair, the larger size being specified first. It should be remembered that a cross should never be described by only three sizes.

Side Outlets: When fittings have a side outlet, their ends should be specified as for normal fittings and then the size of the side outlet should be given. F in Fig. 76 indicates the sequence of the size. For unequal fittings it is best to provide a sketch and indicate whether the side outlet is left or right hand in relation to the other outlets.

Pipe Fitting

In actual practice pipe fitting consists of measuring, cutting, threading, assembling and securing lengths of pipe and fittings. Special tools are required, particularly for threading the pipes, and it is hardly likely that the do-it-yourself will wish to purchase them because they are expensive and are not adaptable for many other purposes. It might be possible to hire tools and equipment from an ironmonger's or engineering works.

MEASURING FOR PIPEWORK

Iron pipes should be fixed about 28 mm clear of the plaster or tiles and due allowance should be made for this when measuring.

There are several methods of measuring and these are illustrated in Fig. 77.

A   End of thread to end of thread.
B   End of thread to centre of fitting.
C   End of thread to back of fitting.
D   Back of fitting to inside of fitting.
E   Centre of fitting to centre of fitting.
F   Back of fitting to end of fitting.

In all cases of measuring due allowance must be made for the engagement of the thread on to the fitting.

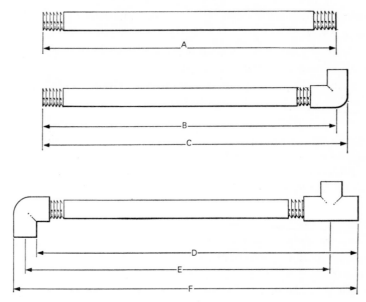

Fig. 77   Measuring for pipework

CUTTING THE PIPES

The easiest way to cut iron pipe is by using special wheel cutters
but the pipe should never be cut completely through with this
tool. It is better to make the final severance with a hacksaw thus
eliminating the internal burr. For pipes of small diameter a good
hacksaw has many advantages. The wheel cutters by their spreading action leave a distinct burr on both the inside and outside of
the pipe and these must be removed by using a file on the outside
and a reamer or rat-tail on the inside. Pipes should never be fixed
without first removing the inside burr. The hacksaw cut leaves
no burrs, but be careful when sawing—the blades break easily
when doing this job.

THREADING THE PIPES

There are a number of excellent stocks and dies available for
threading pipe and although the finished thread made by each

tool is identical, the methods of setting, adjusting and operating them differ.

It may be necessary to file a slight taper on the end of the pipe to be threaded in order to engage the dies, and good 'push-on' pressure is required as the stock is turned. Once the dies start to cut they draw themselves on to the pipe.

It is important, of course, that the dies be engaged perfectly square to the pipe so that the thread will be truly aligned. A lubricant should be applied while the thread is being cut.

After a little experience it will be possible to decide at a glance the correct length of thread.

CONNECTING

Considerable care is required in assembling pipes and fittings, because a faulty joint could give a great deal of trouble and might even mean dismantling the entire system.

Before assembling, the pipes should be inspected to see that the interior is clean and free from any obstruction. If a thread has been cut then be sure that no metal cuttings remain on or inside the pipe. A sharp blow with a hammer will usually dislodge the cuttings.

To make the joint, wipe the oil from the thread with a piece of waste and then fray out the hemp and wrap it round the thread, commencing at the end and following the screw thread. A proprietary jointing paste should then be smoothed over the hemp either with a brush or by fingers.

Next, inspect the fitting to ensure that it is clean and is undamaged and it is a good idea to paint a little of the jointing paste on the thread.

The fitting must engage the pipe thread freely and it should be possible for the first few turns to be made by hand without difficulty. Then a pipe wrench should be used finally to tighten the fitting to the pipe. Gradually increase the pressure on the wrench until the fitting is really tight, but avoid over-tightening, otherwise the fitting might split.

In assembly work some fittings can be assembled in the pipe

vice: others must be fixed in the location in which case two pipe wrenches might be required, one 'holding against' the other.

Beware of a crossed thread in assembly work. This occurs when a fitting is not properly engaged with the pipe. It is easily detected by the sudden tightening of the fitting before more than a thread or two has been engaged.

After making a pipe joint, excess hemp should be removed from the end of the joint. A piece of broken hacksaw blade does this very well. Finally, any marks made by the pipe wrench should be filed off.

PIPE SUPPORTS

All pipework should be supported by projecting clips commonly called 'holderbats'. The back of the holderbat may have a plate with two holes for attaching to a wood ground or may have a tail for building into the wall. The spacing of the supports should be such that there will be no sagging of the pipe, nor any possibility of it swinging on a fitting under its own weight or of being pulled by anyone.

15 | Stainless Steel for Domestic Water Services

Stainless steel tube for plumbing and domestic central heating has now been in regular use since 1966 and to date many millions of feet of tubes of varying sizes have been installed. An all-stainless steel system which will incorporate stainless steel water cisterns, hot water cylinders, tubing and taps is a possibility for the future.

Stainless steel is generally accepted as one of the most corrosion resisting materials available. This resistance is due to the hard, adherent and transparent oxide film that covers the surface of the metal and which re-forms instantaneously if the metal is scratched or abraded. The experience now gained in domestic plumbing confirms that the metal will remain unaffected when in contact with all types of potable water. Because of this immunity there is no danger of corrosion products being formed to contaminate domestic drinking water supplies.

The tube is particularly resistant to damage because of its hardness and high strength and it requires fewer fixing clips and supports than other materials.

The clean attractive appearance of stainless steel tubing and fittings is an important advantage where they have to be fixed in view, although they may be painted without difficulty to blend with any particular colour scheme.

DIMENSIONS AND WEIGHTS OF TUBE

Stainless steel tube for domestic water installations is fabricated by the continuous welding of stainless steel strip. The material used is a stainless steel containing about 18 per cent chromium and 9 per cent nickel.

Dimensions and Weights of Stainless Steel Tube (BS 4127: Part 2)

Size of tube mm	Outside diameter max mm	min mm	Nominal thickness mm	Weight per metre kg	Approx. No. metres per 1,000 kg
6	6·045	5·940	0·6	0·081	12,305
8	8·045	7·940	0·6	0·110	8,965
10	10·045	9·940	0·6	0·140	7,050
12	12·045	11·940	0·6	0·170	5,823
15	15·045	14·940	0·6	0·220	4,601
18	18·045	17·940	0·7	0·310	3,283
22	22·055	21·950	0·7	0·370	2,668
28	28·055	27·950	0·8	0·550	1,829

FITTINGS

The outside diameters of the tubes are such that they can be used in conjunction with fittings specified for the standard copper tube. These fittings are manufactured from copper or copper alloy in accordance with BS 864, Part 2. Stainless steel tubes are suitable for use with capillary and types A and B compression fittings included in this standard. In those parts of the country where dezincification of brass fittings is liable to occur, copper or gunmetal fittings should be used and will be quite satisfactory with stainless steel. As the thermal expansion of stainless steel is very similar to that of copper there is no danger of the joints being weakened through unequal rates of expansion. Where appearance is important chromium or nickelplated copper fittings can be used.

Installation Techniques

CUTTING THE TUBES

A fine-toothed hacksaw (32 teeth per 25 mm) should be used for cutting stainless steel tubes. Standard wheel pipe cutters are also suitable.

BENDING

Because of its ductility the grade of stainless steel tube used for domestic water supply can be bent quite easily by an experienced plumber. The 15 mm tube can be bent by the spring method using the same technique as that employed for copper tubes. The spring should be lightly greased to facilitate its removal after the tube has been bent.

Generally speaking, most bending machines suitable for light gauge copper tube can be used with stainless steel but experience has shown that the higher strength stainless steel requires the use of a sturdier machine than would be necessary for copper tube of similar diameters. For 15 and 22 mm stainless steel tubes it is advisable to employ the bending machines designed for copper tubes of 22 and 28 mm respectively. In cases of doubt the manufacturers of bending machines will be ready to advise.

Jointing

CAPILLARY JOINTS

The procedure is the same as that for copper tubes and fittings (see chapter 13) but because the flux could cause skin irritation it should be applied with a spatula. Also it should be known that the thermal conductivity of stainless steel is low so heat should be applied to the fitting and not the tube.

THE CHOICE OF A FLUX

The extremely high corrosion resistance of stainless steel depends upon its naturally occurring oxide film which re-forms immediately when damaged by abrasion. To remove it by chemical means demands a flux which must be highly corrosive at the moment when the solder is required to wet the steel to make the joint. However, the flux residues remaining after the joint has been made must not be corrosive, and therefore the acid chloride fluxes sometimes used for soldering stainless steel metalwork are not suitable for making capillary joints in stainless steel tube.

The correct fluxes are those based on phosphoric acid. This acid is sufficiently corrosive towards stainless steel at soldering temperatures to provide solder wetting but innocuous after the joint has cooled. These phosphoric acid-based fluxes in paste form, specially prepared for making capillary joints with stainless steel tubes and copper or copper alloy fittings may be obtained from builders' and plumbers' merchants.

COMPRESSION JOINTS

Both type A and type B compression fittings can be used with stainless steel tube and the methods of jointing are explained in the chapter on jointing copper tubes.

STAINLESS STEEL IN CONTACT WITH OTHER METALS

Stainless steel can be used in conjunction with copper alloy fittings and there is no objection to using it in the same circuit as a copper hot water cylinder of a galvanized water tank or cistern. Stainless steel is unaffected by structural materials used in building, such as plaster, concrete and it may be safely embedded in these materials, or brickwork, without fear of corrosive attack. Soil corrosion tests have indicated that stainless steel can be buried underground without suffering any attack and the use of tubes and fittings in this manner has been sanctioned by the British Waterworks Association.

16 | Lead Pipes

Lead is the softest of the common metals and has very high ductility, malleability and corrosion resistance. It is capable of being shaped with the greatest of ease by skilled craftsmen. It does not appreciably work-harden so periodic softening and annealing are not necessary. Lead pipes can be bent into the most complicated shapes thus eliminating much jointing, and tees, crosses, right angle turns, etc., can be made without the use of fittings.

RESISTANCE TO CORROSION

Lead is almost incorrodible and is extremely resistant to town, country and marine atmospheres. It is very seldom corroded by electrolysis when in contact with other metals and in the presence of moisture and it is, therefore, normal practice to use lead with other metals.

Lead is highly resistant to attack from most water supplies. Certain soft waters of acid nature can dissolve small quantities of lead and so make the water toxic, but these are very rare, and in any case the water can be treated to render it harmless to lead.

Some corrosion may occur when lead is in contact with cement mortar or concrete which remains in a moist, fresh state, but not with concrete or mortar that has dried out or aged. Waterproof building paper or other suitable insulating material should be wrapped around the pipes if there is any possibility of direct contact with fresh cement or concrete.

Corrosion of lead can occur if it is in direct contact with timbers when they remain damp or are poorly seasoned. Here again waterproofed paper used to separate the lead from the timber will provide the remedy. Trouble will not arise with well seasoned timber or with well constructed work which will remain dry.

Where there is any danger from atmosphere of certain factories which may contain sufficient acetic acid vapour to cause corrosion of lead, a coat of bitumen will give good protection.

THE STRENGTH OF LEAD

Actually lead is a metal of low strength but in its use provision is made for this and full advantage taken of its other, and unique, properties. Lead pipe has remarkable flexibility which is of great value to permit easy fabrication of plumbing work.

The wall thicknesses of lead pipe required for all normal purposes are quite practical ones and are sufficient to prevent damage.

The fatigue resistance of lead is low and this must be taken into account in its method of use. Fatigue is the tendency of a metal to fail, generally by cracking, when subjected to the repeated application of stress, i.e. reverse bending, alternate heating and cooling, vibration, etc. The fixing of lead pipe is of paramount importance in preventing failure by fatigue.

Soldered Joints to Lead Pipe

WIPED SOLDERED JOINTS

Jointing lead pipes may be broadly divided into two categories; joints to service, supply and distribution pipes of 10 to 40 mm internal diameter and joints to the thinner walled soil, waste and warning pipes from 20 to 100 mm internal diameter.

The traditional method of jointing lead pipe is the wiped soldered joint. The general procedure followed in the preparation, assembly, and the application and control of the solder, is basically similar, both for joints to the smaller diameter supply and distribution pipes, and for joints to soil, waste, vent and warning pipes. Greater control, however, is needed when jointing the larger diameter, thinner walled pipes, in both manipulating the greater mass of hot solder and in applying either the blow lamp flame or hot molten solder to the pipe walls.

To make a satisfactory wiped-soldered joint the plumber must successfully manipulate to a predetermined shape a mass of hot pasty solder which hardens rapidly on cooling. The necessary skill comes from practice.

The outline of the technique of making wiped-soldered joints given here cannot take the place of demonstration and practice, but may prove a useful guide. Some small variations in technique will be found in various parts of the country which it has not been possible to refer to here.

The dimensions of joints and the weights of solder for joints are given to indicate what experience has shown to be average good practice. It is suggested that satisfactory wiped-soldered joints need only approximate to these dimensions and weights, rather than to conform to them accurately.

Table of lengths for wiped soldered joints

Internal bore	Length	Internal bore	Length
mm	mm	mm	mm
10	70	50	80
12	70	65	80
20	70	75	90
25	75	100	90
32	75		
40	75		

Plumber's Solder

The composition of standard plumber's solder is 70 per cent lead and 30 per cent tin with a small percentage of antimony in some qualities, which has a plastic range from 183 to 262°C.

Two methods of applying solder are used, the 'pot-and-ladle' and 'blowlamp' methods. The former is perhaps more suitable for repetition jobs done in the workshops, but the latter is also widely used for shopwork as well as jointing *in situ*. There is, however, no hard and fast rule, and both methods are used for all classes of work.

Characteristics of a Good Wiped-Soldered Joint

The characteristics of a good wiped-soldered joint can be illustrated with an ordinary running joint as an example (Fig. 78A).

(a) A close fit at the meeting ends prevents molten solder running

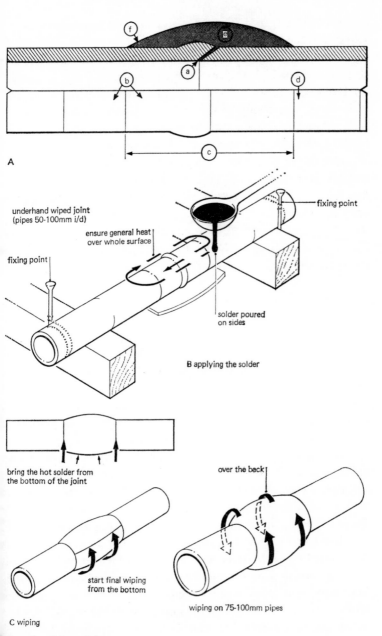

A

underhand wiped joint
(pipes 50-100mm i/d)

ensure general heat
over whole surface

fixing point

fixing point

solder poured
on sides

B applying the solder

bring the hot solder from
the bottom of the joint

over the back

start final wiping
from the bottom

wiping on 75-100mm pipes

C wiping

Fig. 78   Joint wiping

inside. A slight gap at the outer end permits penetration of the solder into the socket to provide a seal.

(b) The area tinned is limited by applying plumber's black to the cleaned and chalked surface of the pipe.

(c) Deep scoring with the shavehook or scriber at the outer end is avoided. The inside of the socket is cleaned. Clean tallow is smeared on the cleaned surfaces immediately.

(d) The cleaned surfaces are completely tinned.

(e) The solder is applied all round in a hot creamy mass with a metallic gleam, and fully molten solder is allowed to be around the junction. Capillary action will draw the solder into the socket to help form a sound joint.

(f) The solder is formed to a smooth curve before it cools to a friable mass ensuring a solid joint. A good joint after cooling shows a bright lustre; a dull joint may be porous.

UNDERHAND WIPED JOINTS

The procedure for preparing an underhand wiped joint with blow lamp or pot and ladle, either on the bench or in a position of easy access, is as follows:

Cut the pipe to length, trim the ends square and remove the burr. Rasp down the spigot for socket entry. Open the socket sufficient for spigot entry and rasp back the surplus edge. Chalk or dust the pipe ends to degrease. Apply tarnish or plumber's black. Measure scribe and shave the ends clean taking care not to cut into the pipe with the shavehook. To give a satisfactory appearance to the joint the scribed line must be at right angles to the pipe. Protect the clean surfaces with tallow. Clean inside the socket, check the entry of the spigot to ensure a close fit. Assemble the joint and fix firmly in position for wiping as shown in Fig. 78B.

When using the pot and ladle, the prepared and fluxed joint is first tinned by gently pouring the molten solder on both the joint and the tarnish at either end to evenly heat the joint area. It is kept flowing in small drips or splashes on either side, and not allowed to run in a stream on the upper part of the pipe (Fig. 78B). Bring up the cooled solder caught in the cloth on to the top of the joint and heat this mass up with hot solder from the ladle. Hot solder should not be allowed to fall from the bottom of the joint, but should be brought up to the top. Try to mould the solder into shape as it is applied, and start the final wiping from the bottom of the joint (Fig. 78c). With a large mass of hot plastic solder the tin-rich solder will tend to drain off the bottom of the joint unless the joint is quickly cooled when completed.

For wiped-soldered joints on the larger-diameter pipes a catch cloth is used to retain the surplus solder, which will run off the joint as the operation of tinning and heating is done, and to mould the solder round the joint. The wiping cloth is used for the final operation. Using the cloth in one hand the plumber moulds the solder at the top of the joint to the required contour. With the edges kept clean the action is continued right over the back, and from slightly above bottom centre the cloth is held at the edges with both hands and brought up to the front to finish at the front near the top (Fig. 78c).

Wiped Joints made with Blow-lamp and Solder Stick

Joint wiping using a blow-lamp and solder stick can, if the proper technique has been mastered, be a very handy method of jointing, particularly in awkward positions or confined spaces. The preparation for the joint is as previously described. The procedure is to heat up the joint and adjacent pipe with the lamp, and to rub the solder stick on the shaved area to tin the surface. As the heat is increased, the solder stick will soften and blobs of solder can be pressed round the joint. In this way the mass of plastic solder is built up all round the joint for manipulation into shape with the cloth. In wiping an underhand joint with the blow-lamp the solder applied to the tinned joint is partially melted and retained in the wiping cloth while playing the blow-lamp continually around the joint mainly to heat the edges and adjacent pipe walls. In moulding the joint, the cloth is first used to lift the hot plastic solder up the front and back to roughly shape the joint. The cloth is then rotated round the joint, applying a slight pressure at the edges and initially a slight side to side movement. This should result in a small surplus of solder being carried round the joint with the cloth to fill up cavities and other imperfections. When the joint is neatly shaped the surplus solder is wiped off lengthwise with a drag-off (folded strip of paper). An advantage of the blow-lamp method is in readily keeping the solder within its plastic range during the wiping operation.

WIPED SOLDERED JOINTS TO BRASSWORK

A joint similar to the underhand joint can be used for jointing brass liners (tail pieces) to lead pipes. These joints are required far more frequently in new work than running or branch joints.

The end of the pipe is prepared as previously described and the liner is tinned. The liner must fit closely into the opened end of the pipe and sufficient distance left between the cap and the end of the joint to allow the cap to be disconnected. The liner is secured to the pipe preparatory to wiping by inserting wooden splints; by grooving the end of the liner and closing the end of

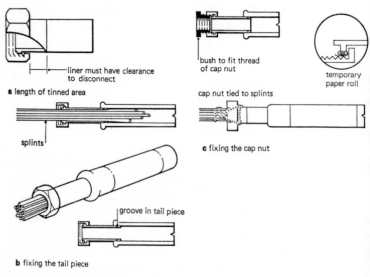

a length of tinned area

liner must have clearance to disconnect

splints

b fixing the tail piece

groove in tail piece

bush to fit thread of cap nut

cap nut tied to splints

c fixing the cap nut

temporary paper roll

Fig. 79   Joints to brass liners

the pipe to grip into it (Fig. 79B); or by burning the liner to the pipe using a suitable flux. The cap nut may be secured by screwing in a suitable bush, or with a roll of paper, which is subsequently removed (Fig. 79C). Alternatively, a purpose made tool, the bur-lock, can be used, which both retains the liner in position and holds the cap.

The pipe is then secured to bench block for wiping the joint when the underhand technique as already described is to be used.

Rolled Wiped Soldered Joints

For jointing brasswork to lead pipe the rolled method is often preferred to the underhand technique, particularly for repetition work. The pipe is carefully straightened and the joint prepared in the same manner. The pipe is then supported on two bench blocks of sufficient height to permit free hand movement beneath the joint. Metal is applied to the prepared joint by blow lamp and solder stick (or pot and ladle) as the pipe is rolled slowly on the bench blocks. When sufficient plastic metal has been built up on the joint and retained in the wiping cloth, the pipe is quickly rolled towards the operative while the cloth is held at the base of the joint with a slight pressure at the edges. The cloth is removed, the joint rolled rapidly back and the action repeated to mould the joint to the required symmetrical shape. Slight pressure on the cloth will remedy any imperfections that appear. Surplus solder is then removed with a drag-off. The joint is immersed, while still hot, into water which gives it a bright lustrous appearance.

WIPED BRANCH JOINTS

The procedure for forming wiped branch joints for 10 to 50 mm bore pipes is as follows:

Cut and rasp down the entering branch to a spigot. Open the pipe with a small drill or pipe-opener and work up the opening to receive the branch (Fig. 80A). Take care to prevent the bent-bolt driving into the inside wall of the pipe and avoid leaving a ridge below the opening. For pipes 32 to 50 mm bore the hole

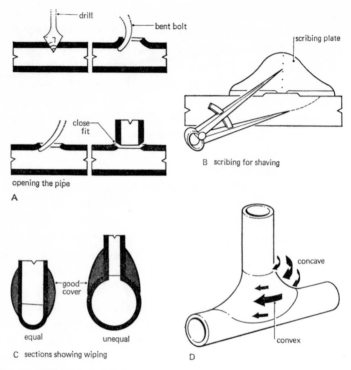

Fig. 80   *Wiped branch joints 10–50 mm*

cut in the pipe for the entering portion is usually less than the inside diameter of the branch. A slight warming of the pipe will assist in forming the opening. Check the entry of the spigot and ensure a close fit. The joint is scribed and shaved, with care not to cut into the pipe (Fig. 80B). The branch is assembled and rigidly fixed for wiping with adequate working space all round. The joint is tinned, then the solder applied to the joint from each side, by blow lamp and solder stick or pot and ladle to obtain a general heat sufficient to maintain the solder in a plastic state. The tin-rich solder that drips down is brought up to the top with the cloth.

In wiping the joint, the top edge is cleaned and the solder is drawn up and round from the base. The pressure on the cloth is changed from the sides to the centre, to leave the joint convex at the sides and concave at the angle (Fig. 80D). There must be enough solder on the side of the joint to provide a good cover.

ALTERNATIVE METHODS OF JOINTING
Bye-laws of water undertakings and local authorities, where they stipulate what jointing method is to be used for water pipe, usually for service pipe laid below ground, normally require that the ordinary wiped-soldered joint be used. There are, however, an increasing number of authorities who permit the use of the soldered spigot joint, which properly made is technically as good, or even better, than the wiped-soldered joint. The soldered spigot joint is made with special but simple tools.

Also, as an alternative to the ordinary wiped-soldered joint the taft or finger-wiped joint is used. Similar to the finger-wiped joint is the cup-and-cone-joint, for which fine solder is used instead of plumber's solder. This joint is generally used for gas pipes Various mechanical joints have also from time to time been put forward for use as alternatives to the wiped-soldered joint, but none has been used except in a very limited way.

The Soldered Spigot joint
The soldered spigot joint is formed by inserting a tinned liner into the prepared end of the pipe, shaped to provide a close fit, and bonding the contact area between the liner and the pipe with fine grain solder. The end of the liner may be slightly chamfered and the outer surface of the liner is tinned prior to insertion.

A suitable solder is one conforming to Grade 'A' of BS 219, which covers an alloy containing 65 per cent tin and 35 per cent lead. The amount of solder used on each joint is very small.

The soldered spigot joint is primarily intended for application to all lead connections to brass tail-pieces in service, supply and distributing pipes. It is also used for running joints and for joints to lead waste pipes up to 40 mm internal diameter. The special tools for making the soldered spigot joint are of a simple type: four coning tools, two cutters, and a set of steel and boxwood mandrels suffice for all average work with 10 to 40 mm diameter pipe of usual wall thicknesses. The hollow wood coning tools are made to different tapers so as to accommodate different wall thicknesses of pipe, and it is necessary to check that the right coning tool is selected to give a suitable taper.

The procedure for making the solder spigot joint is as follows:

First operation—the cutting tool is held firmly in a pipe and gently rotated; any attempt to force it may cut too thick a shaving and make the operation a more strenuous one than it need be. The small end of the cutting tool is filled with tallow to stop shavings falling into the pipe. Shavings are cleared from the cutting tool as the operation proceeds. The inside of the pipe is chamfered down to leave a fine edge of 2 mm or less (Fig. 81A).

Second operation—the specially-shaped steel mandrel is inserted into the chamfered end of the pipe and gently hammered until

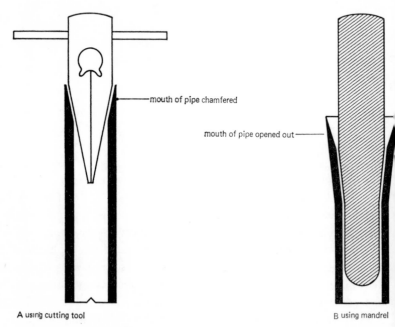

mouth of pipe chamfered

mouth of pipe opened out

A using cutting tool

B using mandrel

Fig. 81   Soldered spigot joint

the pipe is opened to the required depth. The mandrel is smeared with tallow to keep the lead clean. Heat gently applied to thick-walled pipe will greatly assist the opening operations (Fig. 81B). The minimum entry for a service or distributing pipe is 32 mm.

Third operation—a hollow hardwood cone is tapped down over the widened pipe end to shape the sides inwards. Ensure that the end of the socket is tapered evenly (Fig. 81c).

Fourth operation—the tapering of the pipe end is continued until, when tested, the brass liner can be readily, but not loosely, inserted: before the liner is finally inserted its outside surface is cleaned and tinned and the surplus solder wiped off. As not all

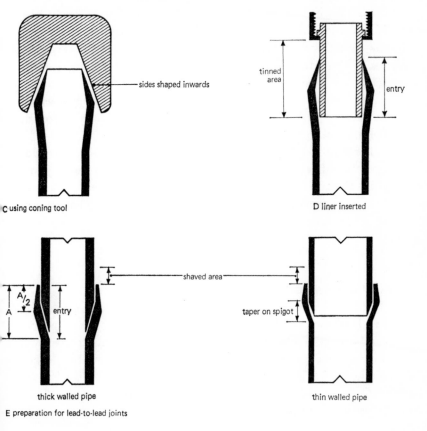

C using coning tool

D liner inserted

E preparation for lead-to-lead joints

brass liners have a perfectly square end, it is an advantage to square off the end with a smooth file and slightly chamfer (Fig. 81D).

Final operation—before introducing the brass liner to the pipe, the top edge of the socket should be neatly filed off, or cut with a knife, to a clean square edge. The liner is then inserted and gently tapped home to ensure close contact at the bottom of the joint. The liner may be slightly smeared with non-corrosive flux paste before insertion.

Heat is gently applied to the liner or spigot part of the joint and then with care to the lower half of the socket. The heat is then mainly concentrated on the brass just above the socket. The solder is applied to one side of the joint and, with the heat spread, it will flow into the bonding area of the joint. When a bright ring of solder is formed all round the shoulder of the joint, gently heat the socket with a moving flame until bubbles of flux cease to rise. The solder will remain molten for a short time, and surplus solder can be neatly wiped off for a clean finish.

For thin-walled pipes, waste pipes and traps it is not essential to use a cutter. Open the pipe with a mandrel for entry and clean the internal surface with a knife or shavehook.

For lead-to-lead joints one pipe end is rasped down to a spigot and the other is shaped to a socket as for lead-to-brass joints (Fig. 81E). When applying heat to lead-to-lead joints a general heat, not concentrated in any one place, is required. The soldered spigot joint is best made in a vertical position.

Taft or Finger-wiped Joint
To make this joint the end of the pipe is 'belled' out by driving in a hardwood cone or turn-pin until the liner or spigot pipe end can be accommodated to a depth equal to about half its diameter. The inside of the pipe end is cleaned and fluxed and the outside blacked. The liner or spigot pipe end is prepared as described for ordinary wiped joints. The joint is firmly fixed and plumber's solder applied and wiped (Fig. 82).

The cup-and-cone joint is similarly prepared, but fine solder (tinman's) is run into the cup to fill it instead of wiping-in plumber's solder.

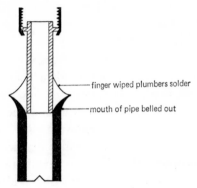

finger wiped plumbers solder

mouth of pipe belled out

Fig. 82. Taft or finger-wiped joint

17 | Roof Weathering

The roofs of homes in this country are usually covered with tiles or slates. Not many new homes have slated roofs because of the very high costs involved. The plumber seldom fixes the roof tiles but he has an important job to do in making the roof watertight.

He is responsible for what is known as the 'weathering', that is the gutters, aprons and flashings which render watertight those parts of the roof where the tiles abut brickwork or pipes. On a modern house roof weathering presents few problems because of the simplicity of design. In many cases, there is but one chimney pot which terminates the flue of the central heating plant. The parts to be weathered are the chimney stack and the soil and vent pipe where it emerges through the tiles.

Weathering a Chimney

No matter how closely fitting the tiles may be to the brickwork where the chimney stack emerges through the roof, they cannot be made watertight without the weatherings. At the back of the chimney there must be a gutter to take away the rainwater as it streams down the roof slope. Down each side of the stack there must be flashings and soakers to keep the driving rain from striking the brickwork and running down into the roof space. The soakers also prevent the discharge from the backgutter from getting through to the roof space, by directing or channelling it towards the roof slope and on its way to the rainwater gutters at the eaves. The front apron protects the face of the chimney stack where it comes through the tiles. Although side flashings with soakers are the most effective method of weathering the sides of the chimney stack, the flashing can continue in one piece from the brickwork on to the tiles. The illustrations show the arrangement of weathering a chimney. This arrangement applies no matter what material is used for the weathering.

The work of preparing and fixing roof weathering is a highly skilled job. The householder should see to it that they are done properly by a skilled plumber because a leaking roof can cause serious damage to property. Do not allow the builder to use cement fillets as a substitute for weathering materials.

Where a soil and vent pipe or a flue pipe penetrates the tiles a weathering is made by means of sleeve, or 'slate', as it is usually called by plumbers. Once again it is stressed that a cement fillet is not suitable.

MATERIALS USED FOR ROOF WEATHERING

Sheet copper, lead, zinc and aluminium are all suitable metals for roof weathering. An asphalt bonded asbestos sheet of laminar construction called Nuralite is now widely used by plumbers. It is highly resistant to atmospheric corrosion and being non-metallic it is not subject to electrolytic decomposition. It is in fact an excellent material for weathering and it costs less than the traditional metals.

The principles adopted in weathering a chimney are the same whatever material is used. The techniques employed in manipulating the materials differ somewhat. For instance sheet lead can be 'bossed' into required shapes by a skilled plumber or it can be cut and welded. Copper can be welted or brazed. Nuralite is manipulated by simple methods and the Nuralite Company Limited, Higham, Nr. Rochester, Kent, will send an excellent instruction manual to any plumber on application.

Zinc is a traditional metal for roof weathering and it is now produced in convenient 10 m rolls in standard widths of 150, 240, 300, 480, 600 mm. It can be worked quite easily and soldered without difficulty. It has been given a trade name of 'Zincon'. The descriptions of the various roof weathering applications are for Zincon but the general principles are similar for all materials.

The weathering applications are shown in Figs. 80 to 90.

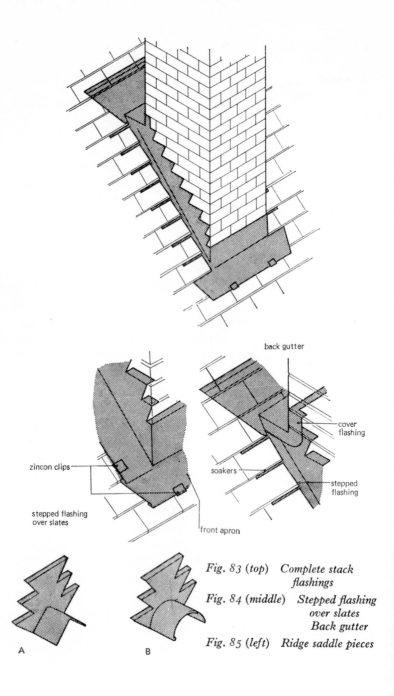

back gutter

cover flashing

zincon clips

soakers

stepped flashing

stepped flashing over slates

front apron

Fig. 83 (top)   Complete stack flashings

Fig. 84 (middle)   Stepped flashing over slates
                     Back gutter

Fig. 85 (left)   Ridge saddle pieces

A   B

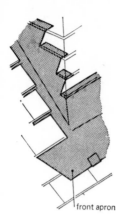

front apron

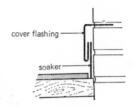

cover flashing

soaker

Fig. 86 (left)   Stepped flashing over soakers

Fig. 87 (above)   Soaker detail

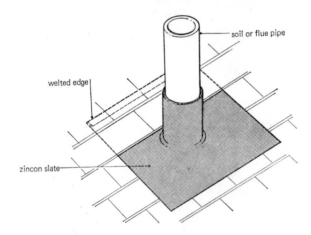

soil or flue pipe

welted edge

zincon slate

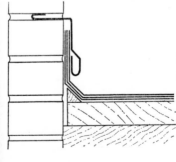

Fig. 88 (above)   Roof penetrations

Fig. 89 (left)   Cover flashing to felt roof

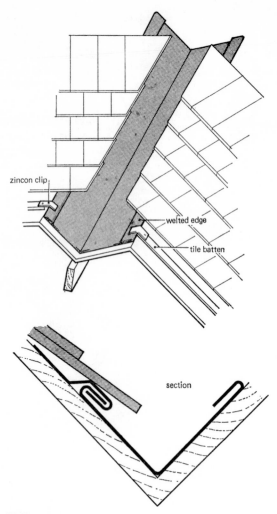

zincon clip

welted edge

tile batten

section

Fig. 90   *Valley gutter*
          Valley gutter section

STACK FLASHINGS

The soft malleable temper of Zincon flashing strip makes stack flashing easy as well as economic. Cover flashings, stepped flashings and front aprons are made in the normal way. Back gutters can be cut and soldered together with no weak spots.

Wedges for joints should be cut from the flashing strip and galvanized nails should be used. No treatment to the surface is needed when bedding the material in mortar joints. Where profiled tiles are used, Zincon can usually be formed into the profile of the tile. Allowance should be made for extra material needed to take up this profile in the case of front aprons.

For deeply profiled tiles it is necessary to cut the strip and tuck it into the profile.

Where chimney stack penetrates the roof at a ridge, the side flashings are joined with a saddle piece. This is formed with a lapped and soldered joint.

Side flashings fixed to brickwork are cut with steps, each step being turned into a joint, wedged, and pointed in. The distance between the internal angle of the step and the line of the roof should not be less than 50 mm and, if the roof covering is plain tiles or slates, the side flashing laps over the upstands of soakers coursed in with the tiles or slates. The soakers are folded to turn up at least 75 mm against the side of the stack and to extend 100 to 125 mm, under the tiles or slates.

The free edge of the flashing is stiffened with a 25 mm fold. Where the roof covering is single-lap tiling or sheet material the flashing extends on to the roof covering 100 to 125 mm. The free edge is secured with 40 mm wide Zincon clips spaced at 300 mm centres and nailed to roof timbers.

Where soil vent pipes or flue pipes penetrate roofs, slates can be easily formed to provide the weather-proofing. The slate is cut to course in with the tile or slate module and a short length of pipe soldered in at the appropriate angle. This length of pipe can be cut and soldered from flat strip. This technique need not be limited to pipe sections and can be extended to roof penetrations of any outline. In the case of flat roofs the same technique should be used except that the slate should be laid over the first layer of felt and under the second two layers.

Felt Roofing
Zincon can be used as a cover flashing where a felt roof abuts a wall.

VALLEYS, GUTTERS AND RIDGE TILES
In new work or repairs it is possible to site form Zincon into valleys and ridges to give a long-lasting job with a pleasing appearance. Valley gutters should be formed with a wooden dressing tool over timber battens. They should be fixed with clips and galvanized nails at 300 mm centres along the edge under the tile or slate. Ridge tiles should also be fixed with clips at 300 mm centres. Overlaps should be 300 mm minimum.

18 | Frost Precautions in the Home

This chapter describes how water pipes and other fittings, including cisterns, should be installed in new houses to be safe from damage by freezing. To improve on existing installations, certain recommendations are given and these, although general, should be practicable in most houses.

HOW TO PREVENT PIPES FROM FREEZING

Obviously prevention is better than cure and the prevention of frost damage to water pipes is not difficult or expensive. If it is understood from the start that if the house is heated the pipes cannot freeze and that if water pipes outside the house are laid in the ground below the penetration of frost they will not be affected, it is clear that the cheapest and most effective method of avoiding frost damage is:

a) Keep the house warm throughout

b) Run pipes in protected places wherever possible

c) If pipes have to be exposed to cold or draughts see that they are protected by efficient lagging

It should be understood that lagging a pipe in an exposed place is inferior to fixing the pipe unlagged in a warm area because it does not matter how thick the lagging, it can only give a limited protection against continued hard frost.

All pipes should be fixed with proper falls so they can be emptied of water when a building is left vacant. Where there is a dip in the pipework that cannot be drained then a draintap should be provided at the lowest point.

WHY SOME BRITISH PLUMBING IS VULNERABLE TO FROST
In most parts of Great Britain the temperature does not fall low
enough every winter to give rise to trouble from burst pipes, and
we never have long periods of exceptionally low temperature such
as occur regularly in Canada or the United States of America
Nevertheless, burst pipes in America are a far less frequent occur-
rence than in this country, a state of affairs arising only in part
from the greater use of central heating throughout that Continent
since full central heating is by no means universal in poorer class
property. Much of the difference arises from the fact that it is
customary to take the rising main up an inside wall (generally
that of the central chimney stack) and to place the cold water
storage cistern with one side in contact with the kitchen or sitting
room chimney flue. This precaution does not necessitate appreciably increased installation costs, for it will be seen from Figs 91
and B that the length of supply pipes is similar in both America
and English practice. (In Figs. 91–95 the heavy arrows indicate
the vulnerable area.) Occasionally it is less convenient for branch
mains, but with a little ingenuity in designing the pipe layout this
can usually be overcome. The only difficulty is that of the tap a

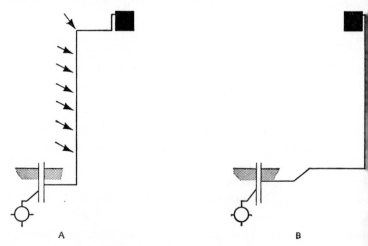

A   B

Fig. 91   Protecting the rising main from frost

the kitchen sink served directly from the main, but this can be connected to the service pipe which runs under the floor with a short length of pipe taken up an inside wall. Figure 92A shows one of several common lay-outs having the advantage of avoiding the usual length of pipe on the outside wall beneath the sink, as in Fig. 92B or just below the sill where conditions are often exceptionally cold. This change in the customary placing of the cold supply pipe will greatly reduce the risk of frost bursts, at any rate in inhabited houses, during normal winters.

WHY PIPES BURST

A study of the action of ice formation which leads to burst pipes suggests other ways in which damage may be obviated. The formation of ice in a waterpipe rarely takes place simultaneously throughout its length, but proceeds progressively from the coldest point towards the warmer points. As is well known, when water freezes its volume increases approximately 9 per cent. If a pipe has one end open and unobstructed, and if ice formation begins at the closed end, it is possible for freezing to continue steadily towards

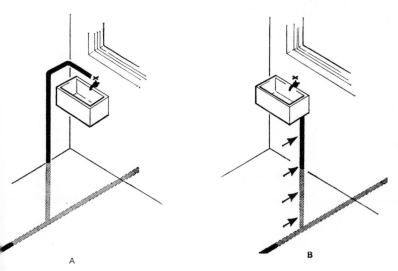

A   B

Fig. 92   The position of the cold supply to the sink

the open end without increasing the pressure on the walls of the pipe, Fig. 93A. Indeed, such a pipe may be repeatedly frozen solid in this way without the slightest risk of fracture. If, however, the freezing begins at the open end (see Fig. 93B) a plug is formed, and as the water cools towards the closed end, pressure is built up until after repeated freezings a burst is inevitable, no matter what thickness of material is used for the walls of the pipe.

In the case of the normal domestic service pipe, the main in the street practically never freezes and so acts as the open end or relief valve, provided always that freezing starts at the remote end. If, however, freezing starts at some intermediate point, and there forms a plug of ice, trouble is likely to be serious between that point and the house end of the pipe. For this reason particular

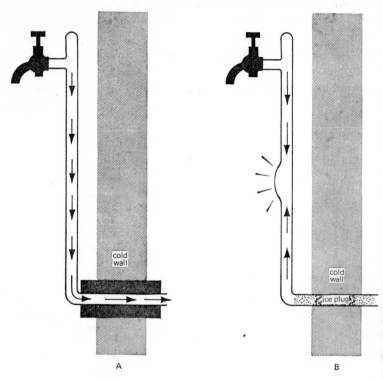

A   B

Fig. 93   Cause of frost burst

care should be taken where it enters the house. It is generally considered in this country that a pipe buried 0·760 m deep in ordinary streets or garden ground is below the limit of frost action, even in severe weather. Again, in the case of a pipe passing over a series of windows or into and out of buildings, there is more than one point likely to freeze and form a plug at a comparatively early stage. In all such cases relatively high pressures will be built up as freezing proceeds from the plug towards the dead end of the pipe and sooner or later a burst will occur.

A pipe buried in an external wall is more likely to freeze than one fixed on the internal surface of that wall since, apart from other reasons, there will be less thickness of wall to protect it. Naturally, too, if it should burst, the damage done to the structure and the cost of repair will be greater.

Pipes which are exposed to cold draughts tend to lose heat rapidly and thus run an increased risk of freezing. Thus, pipes in roof spaces can be protected to a considerable extent simply by covering them with any material which will protect them from draught. Actually, the most vulnerable position for a pipe in a house of normal type occurs at the point where it is carried up the outer wall and passes unprotected close to an open eave, where it is exposed to continual draughts (Fig. 94).

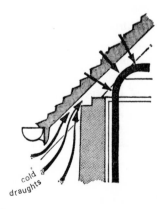

Fig. 94   Exposure at eaves

INSULATION

There are on the market at the moment a great variety of insulating materials, most of which are satisfactory for their purpose. It should be remembered, however, that even the best insulating material must allow of some heat loss, and that during prolonged spells of cold weather it is only a matter of time before the temperature of the pipe falls to a dangerous limit, unless, of course, fresh warmer water is passed through it from time to time. For this reason, therefore, a pipe placed in a wholly exposed position, even after insulation with the best possible material, is not so safe as an uninsulated pipe placed in a room or against a chimney the temperature of which never falls to freezing point for appreciable, periods. Of course, it cannot be guaranteed that the house will not from time to time be left uninhabited, but when this is the case, precautions can and should be taken to see that the pipes are emptied. The boxing-in of pipes in a properly insulated chase generally gives more protection than casual insulation wrapped round the pipe.

PIPES IN EXPOSED POSITIONS

Particular care should be taken when the pipes are placed in exposed positions and protected by insulation to see that all points in the length of the pipe are equally and fully protected, for any part less protected than the rest provides a point at which a plug of ice may form if freezing continues and a volume of water is entrapped between the pipe and a closed end or even another ice plug, increased pressure must occur and there is a risk of bursting.

PROTECTING THE COLD WATER CISTERN

The means commonly taken to protect the cold water storage tank show many examples of wrongly applied insulation. It is common for such cisterns to be protected with an ordinary boarded casing filled with sawdust or some better insulator, but with the feed pipe far less adequately lagged (Fig. 95A). Even if the cistern were to freeze solid, which would take a long time, there would probably be no actual splitting of the metal. The small volume of water in

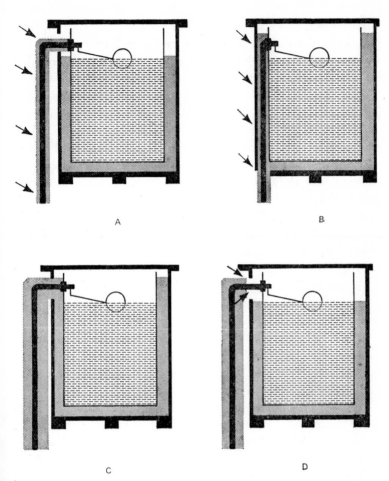

Fig. 95 Insulating the cistern

the feed pipe will, however, not only tend to freeze more quickly, but after several freezings will almost certainly burst the pipe. This, therefore, needs more and not less careful protection than the tank.

Perhaps the commonest mistake where cisterns are thoughtlessly protected is to box-in the feed pipes in the same casing. To some extent, of course, the volume of water in the cistern tends to keep the feed warm, but it will be seen from Fig. 95B that in most cases the amount of effective insulation for the pipe is less than one half that which it has been thought necessary to provide for the cistern. Either the pipe should be separately treated (Fig. 95C) or else an extra space in the boxing of the cistern should be allowed on the pipe side.

Again, it is very common to cut through the casing for a feed pipe without any precautions being taken to insulate the pipe where it passes through the boards or sheeting (Fig. 95D). Such an open hole through the casing and round the pipe may also permit the passage of a considerable draught. This is a very undesirable condition, because, as has been said before, cold air in movement is much more dangerous than air that is completely stationary, which, by the way, is one of the best possible insulating media.

Where any form of organic insulation has been used and trouble is experienced with mice or rats, some protection can be given by wrapping the outside of the insulating material with thin bitumen felt. It is not an absolute safeguard, but appears to be distasteful to most rodents. Moreover, it reduces the passage of air through the insulating material, and prevents accidental wetting, thus giving increased efficiency.

A further point in connection with the use of makeshift insulating materials is in connection with the covering of external waste pipes, particularly from baths and lavatory basins. It is quite common in the country to see such wastes covered with a sack, perhaps straw filled, nailed to the wall above and beneath. When dry this may give some protection. When wet, it is probably worse than useless as the pipe will be surrounded by actual ice, but be effectively shut off from the warmth of the sun in the middle of the day. All insulation must be kept absolutely dry, preferably by boxing-in with a carefully jointed waterproof casing. If this is impossible, then wrapping with waterproof felt will help.

However perfect the insulating material, it is practically valueless when wet, and even when only damp suffers a considerable loss of efficiency.

THAWING OUT

Where through lack of protection lead pipes have been frozen, care is necessary in thawing them out. Even if a burst has not occurred at once because the expansion on cooling has been accommodated by the stretching or give of the pipe, it is quite possible for the trouble to arise later from careless thawing. The warming should be done slowly, starting at the open end of the pipe so that increased pressures are automatically relieved.

Hints to the Householder

It is essential that you should be familiar with your plumbing system, particularly the hot and cold water services. A study of the chapters on these services in this book should enable the householder to cope with an emergency, but if there is any doubt about the draining of the system or if it is safe to use the boiler, then the advice of a qualified plumber should be sought.

THE GOLDEN RULES AT ALL TIMES ARE:

1. Find out where the stopvalve is located.
2. See that it will shut off the main supply.
3. Locate and label any other stopvalves in the house.
4. Repair all leaking taps.
5. Check up on the ball valves of the w.c. cistern and storage cistern in the roof. See that they are not leaking and that they work properly. It will be as well to ensure that the overflow pipes from the cisterns are not obstructed.

WHEN THERE IS A LIKELIHOOD OF A SEVERE FROST LASTING SOME DAYS:

1. Keep the house warm. It takes little heat to keep the water above freezing point. A small lamp or heater will do.
2. Providing the taps do not drip keep the plugs in the waste outlets of baths, sinks, basins.
3. Keep snow and ice from the main stopvalve cover by sprinkling some common salt over it.

4.   Shut the main stopvalve at night and drain off water from the system.

5.   Stop draughts from blowing direct on to pipes and fittings.

6.   A little salt placed in the traps of the sink, basin, bath and w.c. at night will often prevent them from freezing.

IF A PIPE IN THE HOUSE FREEZES:

1.   Shut off the main stopvalve—or if it is controlled by an adjacent stopvalve, shut that off. If the pipe is a distributing pipe from the storage cistern and is not controlled by a valve, inspect it first to see that it has not burst before attempting to thaw it out.

2.   Try to thaw the pipe by using cloths soaked in hot water or safe portable heaters. A blowlamp may be used if the householder is accustomed to its operation. Always start thawing at the nearest open tap on the pipe and work away from it.

IF A PIPE BURSTS:

1.   If the burst is discovered before the thaw begins shut off the main stopvalve; this will stop flooding if the burst is on the main pipe. If the burst is on a distributing pipe from the cistern, close the control stopvalve if there is one. Otherwise open all the cold water taps being fed from the cistern to drain it off as quickly as possible. The main stopvalve must be closed, of course, to cut off the feed.

2.   Call in a qualified plumber as soon as possible.

THE HOT WATER SYSTEM IN FROSTY WEATHER

Many householders get worried in freezing weather about the hot water system of the house, particularly if it is an installation with a boiler. They have heard of boiler explosions in other people's houses. There is little cause for alarm, however, providing normal precautions are taken. In fact it is advisable to keep the hot water system working in frosty weather because the fire—and the pipes— can give that essential background warmth which might well prevent the plumbing becoming frozen.

The essential is that the system is full of water and that none of the pipes are frozen. If a house has been unoccupied for some time during frosty weather and all the pipes are frozen it might prove disastrous to light the boiler fire. If before leaving the house the water has been drained from the plumbing system, including the hot water installation, the latter must be properly refilled before lighting the boiler fire. It is properly refilled when water is running freely from the hot water taps.

It is not advisable for the householder to drain his hot water system without expert advice. Unfortunately, it is not possible to give any general instructions about draining systems, because many have been installed by incompetent persons and an inspection would be necessary before a decision could be made—even by the expert.

If the water from a copper hot water storage cylinder was drained when the vent pipe was frozen, the cold feed valve closed, and the taps at the fitments closed, the cylinder might well collapse like a tin can crushed by a heavy boot. A partial vacuum is caused in the cylinder. When this reduction in internal pressure takes place, the external atmospheric pressure is such that the material from which the cylinder is constructed is not sufficiently strong to withstand the enormous external pressure exerted on the cylinder, with the result that the body of the cylinder is crushed in— or more simply, the cylinder collapses.

19 | Water Softening in the Home

THE ILL-EFFECTS OF HARD WATER

Rain as it falls, particularly over large towns, dissolves carbonic acid gas and other gases in the air; gases carried into the air from factory and household chimneys. So that while rain is the purest form of natural water it is not pure water.

As the rain sinks into the ground it begins to dissolve some of the minerals in the earth and because it has carbonic acid gas in it the rain dissolves some substances more readily. So that when water comes from a spring or from a well—depending to a large extent upon the nature of earth through which it passed originally —it can have dissolved in it a good many different things.

Generally speaking, water that has gone through chalky soil is hard while that which has gone through sandy soils is likely to be soft.

What is hard water? The boy who said that hard water was a chunk of ice and you could soften it by putting it on the hob had got the meaning all wrong. Hard water is so called—so we believe —because it does not easily make a lather with soap. Soft water— as one would expect—is a water which readily lathers with soap.

It is the presence of calcium and magnesium elements in water that hardens it and prevents lather being formed easily. The fat in the soap acts upon these calcium and magnesium elements— upon the hardness—and combines to form an insoluble scum of white curds that float on the water. Put soap in hard water and after a few rubs the water is milky in colour. It gets milkier according to the amount of hardness in the water and number of rubs you give the soap until soap scum—decomposed soap or greasy curdled fat—forms. A lather forms when, and only when, the hardness has been neutralized, but the hardness is still in the water combined with soap and if one washes with water softened by soap, water with the hard scum is still in it, of course.

This scum, because of its sticky nature, clogs the pores of the skin, mats in hair, clings to and discolours clothes and fabrics washed in it and sticks to dishes, silverware and glass. It sticks round washbasins, kitchen bowls, kitchen sinks and baths, in fact it sticks to everything with which it comes into contact.

There are two forms of hardness in water—temporary and permanent. It is necessary to explain the term temporary.

When hard water is heated, some of the hardness is thrown down and evidence of this can be seen in the domestic kettles of homes in hard water areas. That 'fur', or 'scale', is temporary hardness. There are minerals that cannot be removed in this way and substances left dissolved in the water, even after boiling, cause what is called 'permanent' hardness.

When a kettle or a boiler becomes coated with this 'fur', or 'scale', which is a very bad conductor of heat, the water takes longer to boil or requires a great deal more fuel to boil.

Just as 'fur' forms in kettles so it will form around an immersion heater in a hot water tank, in a back fire boiler or in the more conventional free-standing boiler whether gas fired, oil fired, or solid-fuel fired. So also, will it form in the coils of a water heater.

If the hardness is allowed to continue depositing, the immersion heater may well burn itself out or if a complaint is made that the heater has lost efficiency and so has to be removed for descaling, it may well be found that the extent of the scale formation is such that the heater cannot be withdrawn from the tank through the hole originally cut for it, which may well mean the replacement of the hot water tank.

The first sign of trouble is often a complaint from one of the family that the water does not get as hot as it used to or not as quickly as it did. How can it when more and more scale has to be heated before the water itself is heated? In boilers and hot water pipes the scale can thicken and thicken until it chokes off the flow of water and cleaning by a chemical process or complete replacement becomes necessary—an expensive business.

Hard water wastes time, soap and fuel, causes hard work and can in certain circumstances impair health.

THE BENEFITS OF SOFT WATER

Softened water saves soap because only a touch of soap is needed to produce ample lather.

It preserves beauty because it keeps skin soft and supple, as nature intended, keeps pores clean and free, allowing the skin to breathe and improves complexion by eliminating hard water blemishes and prevents 'dishpan hands'.

Softened water improves home laundering because it washes clothes soft and clean, and it is essential for obtaining perfect results with washing machines. It simplifies washing up because it quickly removes grease, and the dishes can be drained clean without wiping. Glassware and silver drain dry to a high polish.

If softened water is used the burden of housework is eased because floors, woodwork, tiles, baths, basins and sinks are quickly cleaned without hard scouring.

Softened water saves tea and coffee because less tea and coffee are needed to obtain the true full flavour and colour.

Plumbing repairs are reduced by soft water because there is no 'scale' to choke the flow in boilers, pipes and radiators—even in car radiators while heated coils last their full life.

The Water Softener

By passing hard water through a water softener, hardness-free water can be obtained. The water from one tap can be softened by using a small portable unit, but for household purposes the ideal unit is one which is connected into the cold main water supply pipe so that all water passes through the softener, and emerges as hardness-free water from every tap in the house.

A water softener is simple to install and maintain and once the softening material in the equipment becomes saturated with hardness, all that needs to be done to bring it back into its original efficiency is to pass ordinary common salt through it. In some models the salt is poured into the container in its ordinary dry form while in the other models—the semi-automatic and the automatic models—the salt is introduced as a brine solution. In either case the salt is rinsed through the softener and once all the salt has gone down the drain the water softener is again ready to give its rated output of hardness-free water. This process is known as regeneration and so long as the water softener is regularly regenerated it will in many years give thoroughly satisfactory service.

The size and type of unit required depends on the degree of hardness of the water requiring to be softened, the number of people using water—for this determines the amount used—and, of course, the space available for the positioning of the unit. They are installed in kitchens, in cloakrooms, in larders, in cupboards under stairs, in garages—in fact in any reasonably accessible position where regeneration can be carried out without difficulty and where easy access can be obtained to water main and drain.

THE WATER-SOFTENING PROCESS

For years household water softening has been undertaken by what is known as the Base Exchange process. The process is virtually the same today, but is becoming more widely referred to as the Ion Exchange method of softening.

A number of ion exchangers are produced in this country and a cation exchanger, a unifunctional polystyrene resin, which is known as Zeo-Karb 225, is used throughout the complete range of the latest household water softeners produced by one well-known company. These ion exchangers have replaced the earlier natural greensand and synthetic materials but the principle of operation remains the same.

Zeo-Karb 225 in its sodium form is used for water softening. A quantity of this material, which is of a golden brown colour and spheroid in shape, is filled into a container and hard water passes through it—generally in a downward direction. The softening material has the unique property of changing its sodium content for the hardness content in the water. In other words, the calcium and magnesium hardness-forming elements in the water are changed into their equivalent sodium elements—nothing more—so that the water contains exactly the same quantity of elements as originally but in another form—in a sodium form. Household water softening is in fact just as simple as that.

Hard water is passed through the resin until it is saturated with calcium and magnesium—saturated with hardness—whereupon the water coming out of the container will be as hard as that going in. The resin is exhausted but as a proof of the further simplicity of household water softening the resin can be brought back to its original condition—to its full water-softening power—by a process known as 'regeneration'.

Sodium must be put back into the resin and what easier way than by passing ordinary common salt—sodium chloride—through it.

Exactly the reverse action to that described takes place. The calcium and magnesium hardness-forming elements are thrown out of the resin which takes up sodium from the salt. The hardness in chloride form is washed down the sink or drain.

WATER-SOFTENING EQUIPMENT

The Portable Unit
The most simple form of household water softener is the portable unit available from good plumbers' merchants and from Permutit Ltd. This is a hard plastics container with polythene handle cap, inlet bend, and outlet spout. A rubber hose is attached to the inlet bend and a rubber connection is pushed on to the tap from which water is drawn. It can be hot water or cold for neither the resinous softening material nor the hard polythene are affected by water temperature.

The softener is delivered already filled with the resin, so that having attached the hose the tap can be turned on. Water enters through the bend on the side of the container and is spread over the resin by means of a distributor pipe. The hard water passes downward through the resin, the exchange previously described takes place and hardness-free water is collected in a pipe at the bottom of the container and passes from the outlet spout under pressure. Turn off the tap and the flow stops.

The quantity of resin in the unit shown is capable of producing 680 litres of hardness-free water providing the hardness of the water is 16°. If there is more hardness in each litre of the water the number of litres softened will be less and, of course, if there is less hardness the number of litres softened will be more.

When the resin is exhausted—or saturated with hardness—the user removes the handle cap and pours into the container 0·50 kg of salt—ordinary common salt—replaces the handle cap and turns on the tap so that the salt dissolves and rinses through the resin until this is regenerated and returned to its original condition.

The manufacturers supply with this unit—and, in fact, with each of their household water softeners—a small simple testing outfit consisting of a shake bottle marked at 40 cc and a bottle of soap solution with a dripper top. With this it is possible to check if softened water is being obtained, that regeneration needs to be carried out or that all salt has been rinsed off. In other words, that regeneration has been completed.

Mains-supply Unit

The portable appliance is an extremely convenient unit for carrying round but the ideal water softener for the householder is a mains-supply unit designed for connecting to the main water supply. In general, the principle of the mains-supply water softener is the same as for the portable unit already described but there are what is known to the manufacturers as dry-salting and wet-salting units.

Mains-supply water softeners are constructed from mild steel plate, which is welded and hot dipped galvanized internally and externally.

ASSESSING WATER REQUIREMENTS

A water softener must be considered against the requirements of the particular household. It is advisable to assess the likely consumption of water, which obviously depends upon the number of persons in residence. In a household where a check was made by a water meter it was discovered that the average consumption of water per person per day, over quite a long period, was 159 litres. This was water for every use and in that particular household nothing but softened water was obtainable. The meter was used not only to check water consumption but also to check the efficiency of the water softener installed. There is good reason to believe this is a fair average consumption of water per person per day, but of course there are households in which the average consumption is higher than this and some where it is lower and it is reasonable to work on this basis. Having ascertained the number of people in residence and multiplied this by 159, it is recommended that the figure should be multiplied again by 8 in order to ascertain the weekly consumption of water in litres. Having arrived at this figure and with the knowledge of the hardness of the water as supplied to the residence, it is possible to determine with reasonable accuracy the size of water softener which is capable of producing at least one week's supply of softened water between each regeneration. A water softener of this size is recommended by the manufacturers, for after long experience they have reached the conclusion that, in the case of manually regenerated water softeners, it is better that regeneration should be undertaken at regular intervals rather than at more frequent intervals. It is better to install a water softener capable of softening more than one week's normal requirements for this then takes into account the possibility of guests or visitors who will, if staying for any period of time, increase the consumption of water. There is no doubt a great deal of harm has been done to the cause of water softening by the installation of units which are quite incapable of producing water in quantity to meet the needs of a household and simplified as regeneration is today, very few people indeed have either the time, or the inclination to undertake regeneration of a water softener every day or every other day. The great difficulty of frequent regeneration is that if the person responsible for it fails to carry out the operation the resinous water-softening material becomes exhausted and the water feeding into the cold water storage tank in the roof and so throughout the water system is as hard as it was before it entered the water softener. Although regeneration will bring the water-softening material back to its original condition so that it immediately produces softened water, unless the whole domestic system is emptied down, it will for some time, depending upon the use of the water, produce what is known as a blended or partially softened water, and if regeneration is required frequently it will appear to the operator that in spite of frequent regeneration, the hardness-free water seldom is obtained, and this of course is a condemnation of the equipment supplies.

CONNECTING THE SOFTENER

To connect these mains-supply water softeners, it is necessary to break into the cold main-water inlet pipe and run what is known as a hard water inlet feed to the water softener and bring a return pipe from the water softener to the main-water-supply pipe and fit between these two connections a valve which becomes known as the by-pass valve, and which of course is closed when the water softener is in operation. Some manufacturers recommend a valve should be fitted on both the hard water inlet and soft water outlet lines purely for emergency purposes. By fitting these you enable the owner of the equipment to completely isolate the water softener, if, for instance, they leave, or let, the house for some time and have somebody living in it whom they do not wish or who does not wish to undertake regeneration. Furthermore, if the owner wishes to disconnect and take away his water softener, perhaps for installation at another address, by the fitting of these emergency valves this can be carried out without great difficulty. Some water companies insist upon the fitting of a non-return valve before the water softener and local knowledge should be used or the position ascertained in determining whether or not to follow the manu-facturers' recommendation. A waste pipe is required in order to take the effluent during regeneration away to an outside gully or drain and the size of this waste pipe should be determined by the size of the hard water inlet pipe and, of course, of the length of the run of the waste and whether or not it contains a number of bends and elbows.

20 | Flushing Cisterns Explained

A fixed quantity of water must be discharged to cleanse water closets and for this purpose flushing cisterns are used. A cistern is stipulated for the following reasons:

1. To provide sufficient water to flush and cleanse the pan effectively and reseal the trap with fresh water.

2. To prevent waste of water by using a regulated volume to each flushing.

3. To break direct contact between the water supply and the fixture so that, should a stoppage occur in the fixture, the pollution of the water supply by foul water being siphoned back into the main will be prevented.

The flushing cistern generally used is known as a valveless, waste water preventing, siphonic cistern, so called because there is no valve through which water from the cistern can run to waste down the flush pipe and because the discharge of water is due to siphonic action. Although flushing cisterns differ in design and construction, most of them depend upon the principle of siphonage for the discharge of their contents. The cistern has provision made for the supply of water through an automatic ball valve situated either on the right hand or left hand side. On the opposite side, provision is made for the connection of an overflow pipe which allows excess water where it will be noticed, but will not cause a nuisance or damage property. The flush pipe connection is at the bottom of the cistern.

It is only necessary in this description of flushing cisterns to deal with two types (1) a straight outlet cistern and (2) a low level cistern, both of which are in common use in normal houses.

STRAIGHT OUTLET CISTERN

Construction

This type of cistern has the working parts contained in a cast iron vessel, with a cylindrical well in the centre of the bottom. In this well is a vertical outlet pipe with a lip at the weir and an enlargement near the bottom, to assist in the setting up of siphonage. The outlet pipe weir terminates slightly above the normal overflow weir of the cistern.

A heavy cast-iron bell of conical shape, flared out at the bottom, fits over the outlet pipe and stands in the well. It has a diameter at the base which allows it to move up and down freely in the well, but has only a small space between it and the wall of the well.

The bell has a loop at the top to which is attached a lever and a chain, and near the bottom is a small air break hole. Projecting lugs leave a clear space between the bottom of the bell and the bottom of the cistern.

In this type of cistern, as shown in Fig. 96, a simple inverted U-tube is formed, the short leg being the annular space between the outlet pipe and the inside of the bell, and the long leg being the outlet pipe and its continuation as a flush pipe.

Water is supplied through an automatic ball valve which should be adjusted to shut off when the water level is about 25 mm below the overflow weir of the tank.

Action

Figure 96A shows the cistern ready for discharge, the bell in its normal position and the automatic ball valve shut off, the water level being the same under the bell as in the cistern. Air which previously filled the space between the bell and outlet pipe has now been expelled through the outlet pipe as the water has risen. The bell is raised by the lever and chain (B), but actual siphonage is not set up until the bell is lowered.

On release of the chain the bell, owing to its weight, drops heavily on the water beneath it, which cannot escape quickly enough through the small space between the bell and the vertical wall of the well. It is compelled to rise inside the bell and flows

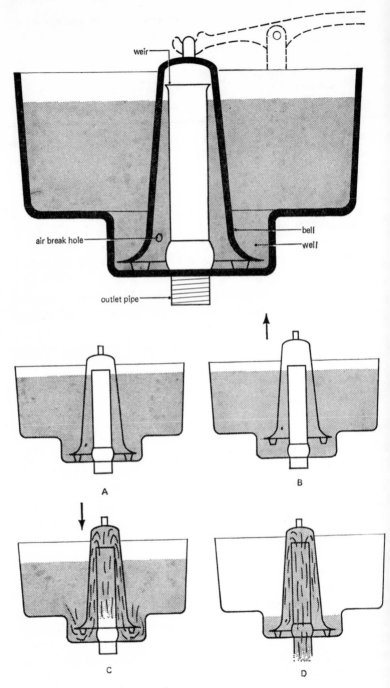

Fig. 96   *Flushing cistern action*

over the outlet weir and down the long leg of the U-tube, thus setting up siphonic action, as shown in (c). This siphonic action will continue until the level of water is reduced to the air hole in the bell, as shown in (D), when an admission of air breaks the siphon and allows the cistern to fill again.

LOW-LEVEL CISTERN

A low-level cistern is generally part of a suite, consisting of cistern, flush pipe and pan, designed for the efficient working of each part and a relatively silent flush.

Construction

The vessel of the low level cistern, as shown in Fig. 97, is of heavy glazed pottery ware. Although it contains the usual quantity of water it has a comparatively small width, thus taking up a minimum of space. An inverted U-tube is formed in the cistern, a straight 45 mm diameter pipe and the flush pipe forming the long leg.

The short leg is formed by the inlet pipe in the cistern near the bottom. There is no bell in this cistern, but a balanced plunger is fixed inside the inlet to the U-tube and rests on a rubber-coated rod.

The plunger is connected by levers to a small turn handle fixed on the outside of the cistern. All these parts are made of heavily galvanized iron to prevent the formation of rust.

Connected to the crown of the U-tube is a small brass air pipe which terminates about three inches from the bottom of the cistern. Its function is to admit air to stop the siphonic action at the conclusion of the flush. The weir of the U-tube is situated above the overflow weir of the cistern, and in this regard a similarity to the straight outlet type of cistern will be observed.

As the height at which the cistern is fixed has a direct bearing on the proper flushing of the pan, it is important that the length of the flush pipe should not be altered by the plumber when fixing the suite. The loss of head of water by fixing the cistern at a low level is offset by the increased diameter of the flush pipe.

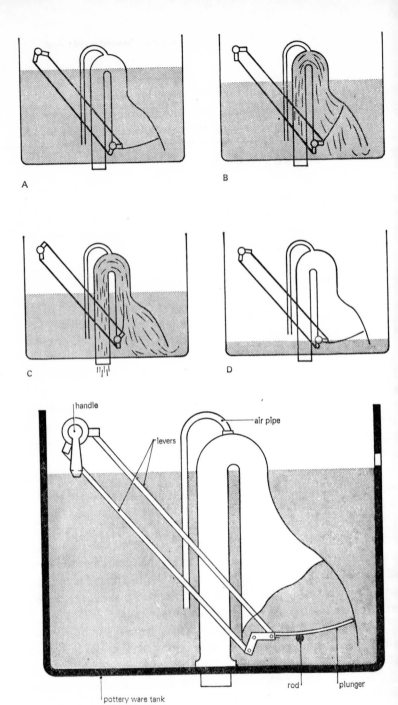

A

B

C

D

handle

air pipe

levers

pottery ware tank

rod

plunger

Fig. 97   The low-level cistern

Water is supplied through an automatic ball valve which should be adjusted to shut off when the water is about 25 mm below the overflow weir.

Action

As the long leg of the U-tube is open to the atmosphere the water flowing into the cistern will rise in the short leg of the U-tube to the same level as that in the cistern, as shown in Fig. 97.

Siphonage is set up by turning the handle on the outside of the cistern. The balanced plunger is thrown upwards, causing a wave motion of the water in the U-tube, as shown at (B).

This results in a quantity of water being forced over the weir of the inverted U-tube, and down the long leg causing siphonic action to be set up, such action continuing as shown at (C).

When the level of water in the cistern has been reduced to the inlet of the air-breaking tube, an admittance of air breaks the siphon, as shown at (D).

Owing to the plunger being balanced, it will remain in an upward position during the time the water is discharging from the cistern. As the discharge finishes, it will slowly come to rest on the rubber-coated rod, in its original position.

Fault Finding, Repairs and Maintenance

Faults in Ball Valves

Cause	*Remedy*
Rubber washer worn or defective.	Renew rubber washer.
A piece of rust or other foreign matter on the rubber washer, preventing the washer from fitting correctly on its seat.	Remove the foreign matter or Rewasher the valve.
Ball water logged, and instead of floating on the surface of the water remains partly or completely submerged; therefore there is not sufficient power to lever the rubber washer to its seat.	The ball must be drained of water and repaired where defective, or Renew the ball.
Ball detached from lever. Incorrect adjustment of the lever.	Re-attach ball to the lever. The lever arm should be bent down at the ball end so that the rubber washer is forced to its seating when the water level is lowered.
Jamming of the ball on some portion of the cistern.	Free the ball and adjust the lever arm to prevent recurrence of the trouble.
The seating of the valve defective and not providing a proper surface for the rubber washer.	Seat of valve may be re-faced or The body of the valve or the complete ball tap replaced.
Striking arm of the lever in the plunger worn.	File where bearing or Renew lever arm.

RE-WASHERING A BALL VALVE

1. Shut off water supply at the stop tap.

2. Disconnect the union nut between supply pipe and ball cock.

3. Unscrew the lock nut and remove ball cock from cistern. Should the ball cock have a cap piece, as shown in Fig. 98, it is unnecessary to remove the ball cock from the cistern as the cap and split pin may be removed without removing the complete ball valve.

4. Remove the split pin to release the lever arm and plunger.

5. Disconnect the extension and valve seating from the body, by using a pipe wrench or spanner on the hexagonal shoulder and holding against the pressure with a rod placed in the water outlet.

6. Take the plunger apart by inserting a flat tool in the lever arm slot, and unscrew the cap piece with pliers or a small wrench.

7. Remove the old rubber washer and clean away any rubber adhering to the cap piece or plunger.

8. Cut a piece of rubber to size and insert it in the plunger cap piece. When a washer is to be cut, place the cap piece on the rubber and give it a light tap. This will mark the correct outline of the circle to be cut. Cut the rubber neatly with the wet blade of a knife and then insert in the plunger cap piece.

9. Screw the cap piece on the plunger and tighten. The rubber washer may have a very slightly convex facing to the seat, as shown in Fig. 98. If the washer is too thick, or cut too large, the facing will be too convex (B) and the washer will not last long.

10. File any tool marks off the plunger and place it in the body.

11. Insert the lever arm in the plunger slot, and secure the plunger and lever arms by replacing the split pin and opening its ends.

12. Screw the extension and valve seat tightly to the body.

13. Replace the ball cock in the cistern.

14. Tighten the lock nut and connect the union nut on the service pipe.

15. Turn on the water supply.

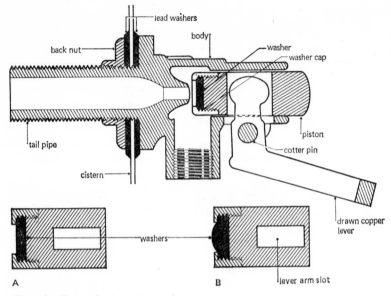

Fig. 98   Re-washering a ball valve

THE BRS BALL VALVE SHOWING WORKING PARTS

The ball valve illustrated in Fig. 99 was designed by the Department of Scientific and Industrial Research (Building Research Station) to fulfil the urgent need for fittings which would give longer, reliable service, and not be prone to the well known weaknesses of earlier types. We refer, of course, to the corrosion or erosion of the metal seatings which results in the familiar 'saw-cut' effect, and to the sticking of the piston of Portsmouth type valves in certain waters. These disadvantages have been fully overcome, and in the latest design several other most desirable features have been included.

The main features of the BRS Ball Valve are as illustrated, a nylon nozzle shaped to overcome cavitation and a rubber diaphragm which stops the flow of water when pressed against the nozzle by a plunger. This design ensures that the moving parts of the valve are out of water and therefore free from corrosion and incrustation. The movement of the plunger is controlled by the usual float on a hinged arm, which at its free end is bent

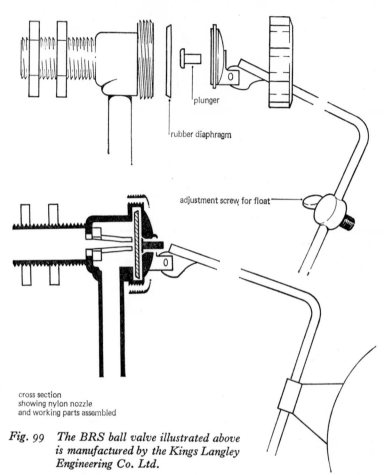

plunger

rubber diaphragm

adjustment screw for float

cross section
showing nylon nozzle
and working parts assembled

*Fig. 99   The BRS ball valve illustrated above
is manufactured by the Kings Langley
Engineering Co. Ltd.*

down at a right-angle. By means of a thumbscrew, the float can
be fixed on this part of the arm at any height depending on the
water level required in the cistern. It can also be adjusted radially
to avoid any obstacle.

RENEWING A TAP WASHER
Step by step
1.   Turn off the supply to the tap at the stopvalve.
2.   Open the tap to its fullest extent and unscrew the easy-clean
shield to expose the hexagon on the headpart (Fig. 100A).

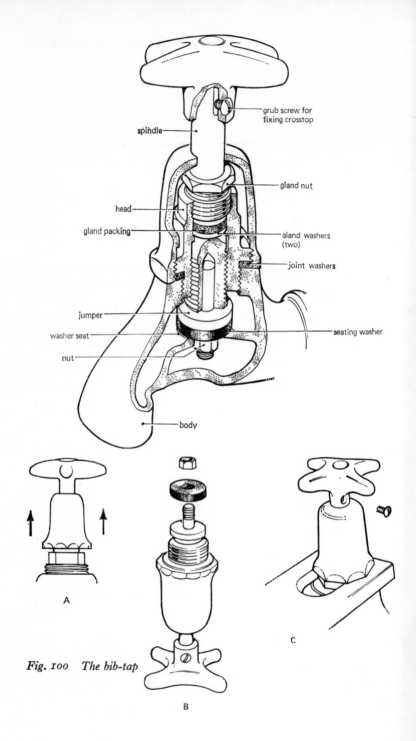

grub screw for fixing crosstop

spindle

gland nut

head

gland packing

gland washers (two)

joint washers

jumper

washer seat

seating washer

nut

body

A

B

C

Fig. 100   *The bib-tap*

3. Using a spanner unscrew the headpart from the body of the tap. The body of the tap should be firmly held with the free hand against the pressure exerted by the spanner.

4. Release the worn washer by removing the nut holding the washer to the jumper (Fig. 100B).

5. Replace the washer making sure that it is the correct size for the tap jumper, and tighten the retaining nut.

6. Replace the headpart and tighten with spanner, again holding the free hand on the tap against the pressure exerted by the spanner. Make certain that the spindle of the tap is still in the open position, otherwise the washer will engage the seating of the tap and prevent the headpart being screwed tightly on the body.

7. Restore the water supply by opening the stopvalve.

REPACKING THE GLAND
Step by step

1. Remove the grub screw securing the crosstop (see Fig 100C) and turn the tap fully on to expose as much of the spindle as possible.

2. Unscrew the easy-clean shield and raise it to expose the hexagon head of the tap.

3. Insert a piece of wood or two spring type clothes pegs (Fig. 100C) to keep the shield in the raised position. Close the tap and the crosstop will be removed by the upward pressure of the easy-clean shield.

4. Unscrew the gland nut, remove the top washer and pick out the defective gland packing.

5. Re-pack the gland with lamp cotton into which vaseline has been worked. Make two or three turns of the cotton around the spindle in a clockwise direction, pressing it down into the gland box.

6. Replace the top washer and screw down the gland nut firmly.

7. Before replacing the easy-clean cover slip on the crosshead and turn on the tap to ensure that the packing is effective. If it leaks a little, take another turn on the nut.

Faults in Screw-down Taps

Defect	Cause	Remedy
Water flowing or dripping from the tap outlet when shut hard down.	Worn or defective washer. Piece of grit, rust or other foreign matter on the washer. Defective seat of tap.	Re-washer tap. Remove foreign matter or Re-washer tap. Renew tap.
Water flowing from around spindle or stuffing box screw.	Defective packing in stuffing box. Screw of stuffing box not screwed down tightly.	Renew packing with greased hemp. Tighten stuffing box screw.
Spindle continually slipping when turned and tap will not shut off.	Spindle thread stripped or badly worn.	Renew tap. Renew packing with greased hemp.
Tap hard to turn on and off.	Stuffing box packing too tight. Spindle bent.	Work tallow into stuffing box. Renew tap.
Loud noise in the tap when turned on.	Valve loose on the spindle. Washer loose on valve.	Solder the valve to the spindle or Renew tap. Renew the valve or washer or Renew tap.
Sudden cessation of the flow of water.	Foreign object caught in the stop cock ferrule, stop tap, or a particular tap.	Shut off water and clean out the obstruction.
Stain from water on sanitary fitment.	Stain from leather washer on valve.	Replace leather washer with a fibre washer.

CARE OF CHROMIUM PLATED FITTINGS

Water fittings are usually made from brass, an alloy of 60–65 per cent copper and 35–40 per cent zinc. The component parts are either made from brass rod, brass tube, brass castings or brass forgings. After all the machining operations are carried out the surface is usually ground and polished, which makes it easier to keep such fittings clean.

Although brass-polished fittings look very nice this metal tends to tarnish very quickly, and whilst grandmother had plenty of time and was prepared to clean her water tap at least once a day most carefully, today there are so many taps, mixers and shower fittings in the house, the cleaning of which would occupy a housewife's day completely. In consequence good quality water fittings are nickel-plated, which is comparable with a good priming or undercoat and subsequently chromium-plated, which is the top high-gloss finishing coat.

Chrome is extremely hard and resistant to most acids. All that is necessary is to wipe the fitting dry immediately after use and if this is done regularly, fittings will last a lifetime. However, the majority of people are much too rushed nowadays and cleaning of chromium-plated fittings takes place when they look dull and dirty. 'Elbow-grease' is a rare commodity and modern cleaning agents are being used. One could classify such materials into four groups:

1. Steel wool or plastic scourers which are frequently impregnated with alkalines and solvents.
2. Cleaning agents containing fine pumice and bleach.
3. Grease-dissolving materials mainly recommended for washing crockery.
4. Washing powders containing a host of complex chemicals.

All the aforementioned cleaning materials combine in the worst case, harsh abrasives with chemicals, and in the best case chemicals only. It therefore stands to reason that frequent use will gradually destroy the protective coating and the life of a chromium-plated water fitting and its glossy, brilliant surface will last from six months to 20 years, depending on the treatment it receives.

FITTING A WASTE OUTLET TO BATH, SINK OR WASHBASIN

The method of performing this operation is as follows:

1.   Remove the lock nut from the thread, and cut a sheet lead or plastics washer to fit over the thread (Fig. 101A).

2.   Paint the outside of the plug and washer, and around the inside and outside of the outlet hole of the fixture, with white lead paint.

3.   Fill the flange of the plug with a mixture of white lead (or white lead oil) and linseed oil putty, and, with a few strands of hemp wound around, insert through the outlet hole (Fig. 101B).

4.   Paint the lead washer, and with a little of the putty mixture on it place it over the thread of the plug, and tighten firmly with the lock nut (Fig. 101C). When fitting a plug and washer to a fixture with an overflow, a grummet of hemp should be placed between the sink and the lead washer to prevent the putty mixture being squeezed into the overflow holes of the plug and washer.

5.   Adjust the grating bars to a neat finish and clean off surplus putty and paint.

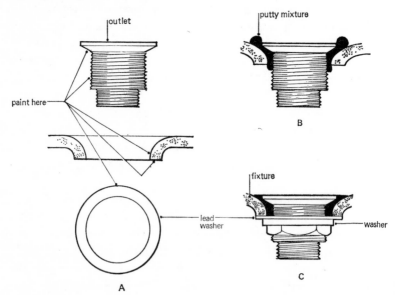

Fig. 101   Fitting a waste outlet

STOPPAGES IN WASTE PIPES

Stoppages in waste pipes are indicated first by a slowing down of the usual rate of discharge of waste water, and finally by a complete stoppage of the discharge. The position of a stoppage may be at any point between the fixture and the point of discharge to the drain, and is caused generally by a gradual silting up of the pipes with matter carried by the waste water. A stoppage usually occurs at fittings, particularly when the burr has not been removed from the pipe after cutting, and also in long runs of pipe with insufficient fall. If effective gratings are fitted on fixture outlets, stoppages caused by foreign objects in the pipes are rare. If foreign objects do pass the fixture grating, they will generally be found in the fixture trap. The trap may be cleaned by removing the cleaning screw (Fig. 102).

In modern plumbing systems the trap beneath the kitchen sink and washbasin in the bathroom will often be of the type that can be dismantled without difficulty. This enables the U part of the trap to be cleansed and also allows access to the waste pipe.

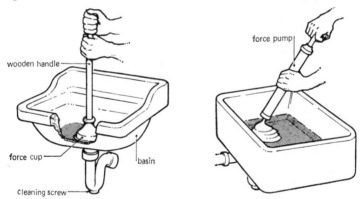

wooden handle

force pump

force cup

basin

cleaning screw

Fig. 102   Clearing a stoppage in a waste pipe

CLEARING STOPPAGES IN WASTE PIPES

Choked waste pipes may be cleared either by the application of suction and pressure, or by using wires or canes. Where compressed air is available it may be used to bring direct pressure to bear in clearing stoppages.

SUCTION AND PRESSURE

Force cups and force pumps are used for creating suction and pressure on stoppages in waste pipes.

Force Cups

A stoppage in a single fixture may be cleared by using a force cup, as shown in Fig. 102. A force cup consists of a rubber cup with a wooden handle, and is placed over the outlet of the fixture and worked with a reciprocating action, thus causing suction and pressure in the waste pipe. Force cups are particularly useful for stoppages in lavatory basins.

Force Pumps

A patent force pump with a rubber cap and a pump attached is also used for waste pipe work.

22 | Home Improvement Grants

Over a million and a quarter older homes have been modernized, mainly in respect of bathroom facilities, with the aid of house improvement grants since the system was introduced in 1949.

But thousands of homes still lack modern amenities. In fact, it has been estimated that there are nearly two million homes in England without a bath, let alone an inside w.c.

Assistance for people who want to improve and modernize older homes in sound condition was increased by the Housing Act, 1969. The main obstacle, however, is a lack of knowledge by the general public of just what they are entitled to under the grants and how they go about getting it.

There are three types of grant available through local councils, the main one being the standard grant for the provision of certain amenities in existing dwellings. Standard grants are made to help meet the cost of improving houses by providing, for the first time, a fixed bath or shower in a bathroom; a wash-hand basin; sink; hot and cold water supply at any of these; and a water closet.

The council will meet half the cost of the improvement works—including professional fees—if certain conditions are fulfilled. The house must have been built before October, 1961; it must already be in a good state of repair, and remain habitable for a further 15 years; the standard amenities must be for the sole use of the occupants.

These grants are subject to a normal maximum of £200 for providing all five improvements, made up as follows:

Supply and fix:

Bath or shower	£30
Hot and cold water to bath/shower	£45
Wash-hand basin with hot and cold supply	£30
Toilet	£50
Kitchen sink with hot and cold supply	£45
	£200

Sometimes it is not practicable to provide a bathroom except by building on to the house, or converting outbuildings attached to it. In these cases an equal amount to half the reasonable cost will normally be substituted for the allowance of £30.

If the council is satisfied that it would not be possible or practical to provide a w.c. and connect it to main drainage, and the w.c. is to be installed with septic tank or cesspool drainage, again half the reasonable cost will be substituted for the normal allowance of £50.

Where a supply of cold water has to be brought into the house to carry out the improvements, an additional amount equal to half the normal cost of this work can be included in the calculated cost of the maximum grant.

If all or any of these circumstances apply, the grant is subject to an overall maximum of £450 instead of the normal £200.

The council may be prepared in some circumstances to allow a grant even when all the amenities will not be provided. For example, if the council are satisfied that it would not be practicable at reasonable cost to improve the house to full standard, and that, at least after the improvement, the house will be provided with a sink, hot and cold water supply and w.c.

A standard grant can also be made available for repairs if the householder agrees to carry out, at his own expense, and repairs which the local council regards as necessary.

Although drawings do not have to be submitted to the council
under the standard grant, check that the grant application has
been approved before starting work. Disqualification from assistance can happen if work starts before approval has been given.
Approval for building regulation or planning purposes is not the
same as grant approval.

A point worth noting is that, to ensure prompt payment on
completion, all estimates should be as accurate as possible covering
all contingencies.

The other types of grant available through local councils are
discretionary grants and special grants.

Discretionary grants are for thorough improvements to a high
standard or for providing dwellings by conversion. The council
may pay for these at their discretion and will meet up to half of
the estimated cost of modernization (including professional fees).
This grant is normally made for works costing upwards of £100,
with a maximum of £1,000 for each house improved or for each
living unit improved by conversion. (Example: 3 flats—up to
£3,000).

Special grants are a new kind of assistance, for the provision of
basic amenities for the overall benefit of houses in multiple occu-
pation. This grant is also payable at the discretion of the local
authority, and the basic amenities and amount of the grant are
the same as for standard grants.

If there is any doubt regarding grants, details are readily available from the local grants officer for each borough or town, who
will also advise on any local stipulations.

Index